# THE 24/7 CHRISTIAN

# The **24/7**
# CHRISTIAN

practical help from the book of James

Anthony Selvaggio

EVANGELICAL PRESS

EVANGELICAL PRESS
Faverdale North, Darlington, DL3 0PH, England

e-mail: sales@evangelicalpress.org

Evangelical Press USA
P. O. Box 825, Webster, New York 14580, USA

e-mail: usa.sales@evangelicalpress.org

web: http://www.evangelicalpress.org

First published 2008


British Library Cataloguing in Publication Data available


ISBN-13   978-0-85234-687-7                    ISBN  0-85234-687-5

Printed and bound in the United States of America.

*I dedicate this book to my son James.*
*May he pursue divine wisdom all the days of his life,*
*and may he endeavour to be worthy*
*of the title given to the Lord's brother*
*— 'James the just'.*

# Contents

# 1.

# James the man

*'James, a servant of God and of the Lord Jesus Christ'*
(James 1:1).

In many ways, James is the forgotten epistle of the New Testament. Throughout church history the epistle of James has encountered struggle, opposition and just plain neglect. In the period of the early church, it struggled to receive full acceptance in the canon of Scripture. At the time of the Reformation, it faced fierce opposition, particularly from the great Reformer Martin Luther, who dismissed the epistle outright, referring to it as an 'epistle of straw'. He also charged that James 'mangles the Scriptures and thereby opposes Paul and all Scripture'.[1] In our modern age, James has suffered from both lay and scholarly neglect. When it comes to the New Testament epistles, the writings of Paul, Peter and John garner most of the attention, while James and his epistle have been largely ignored throughout history.

This is unfortunate, because it has much to say to us — particularly regarding the crucial subject of the Christian life. Perhaps no other letter in the New Testament so comprehensively addresses the Christian life as does the epistle of James. It is the purpose of this book to explore the Christian life through the panoramic lens of this grand epistle.

Before we begin our exploratory journey through the epistle of James, it will be helpful to first properly prepare and equip ourselves for this journey. Just as a hiker ensures that he fills his backpack with the basic necessities and tools needed for a successful hike, we too need to fill our theological backpacks with some basic information to ensure our journey through James is profitable. What do we need to know about James to have such a successful journey? We need to know some basic details about James the man who penned this letter. God used real people with real personalities as instruments of inspiration. James was a real man and, as James Adamson notes, his 'Epistle is alive with the personality of its author'.[2] Therefore, knowing something about James the man will help us to understand his letter. Who was this James? What do we know about his life? Let's unravel the mystery of James the man.

## Who was this James?

It is the general pattern of the New Testament epistles to open with a greeting in which the author identifies himself. James follows this pattern by identifying himself as 'James, a servant of God and of the Lord Jesus Christ' (James 1:1). Unfortunately, this greeting does not tell us much about James. There is nothing here about his family relationships or his position in the church. All he gives us is his first name. This generic greeting has frustrated biblical scholars, because the name 'James' was quite common in the ancient world. In fact, there are six different men named James in the New Testament alone![3] It would have been extremely helpful had James told us which James he was, but he didn't.

Our inquiry, however, has not reached a dead end. While James failed to tell us which James he was in his opening statement, the rest of his letter leaves little doubt regarding his identity. The epistle of James reveals that its author is none other than James, the Lord's brother. How does the epistle support such a conclusion?

Proving that the author of this epistle is James the Lord's brother requires a bit of detective work. Let's say one day you discovered an ancient letter in your attic. The contents of the letter were quite intriguing, but the author failed to identify himself. However, from the contents of the letter you were able to determine that the author was male and one of your five uncles. You could then determine which uncle wrote the mysterious letter by comparing its vocabulary and style to other known writings from your five uncles.

A similar thing can be done with the epistle of James. While we do not have another full-length epistle written by James the Lord's brother, we do have an inspired sample of his speaking patterns preserved for us in the Acts of the Apostles. In Acts 15:13-29, the Lord's brother gives a speech at the Jerusalem Council which was recorded by the conscientious Luke, the author of Acts. When one compares the vocabulary and style of this speech to the epistle of James the similarities are both striking and convincing.[4] This comparison leaves little doubt that the man who gave the speech in Acts 15 also wrote the epistle of James.

In addition to this internal biblical evidence, we also have external evidence which supports the conclusion that the epistle was written by the Lord's brother. Numerous church fathers — including Origen, Eusebius and Jerome — testify that it was James the Lord's brother who wrote it. The chronology of James' life and the audience of the epistle also serve to support this conclusion.[5] Although the authorship of this epistle is still a matter of much scholarly contention, when all the evidence is weighed the argument for James the Lord's brother clearly prevails.

However, if the author of this epistle is the Lord's brother, why didn't he simply identify himself as such in the opening of his letter? After all, it would seem to be a way to gain instant credibility with his audience by linking himself to Jesus. What can explain the generic greeting found in James 1:1?

There are two possible explanations. James may have chosen not to mention his relationship with Jesus to demonstrate his humility. Alternatively, he may have failed to mention it because it was simply unnecessary. Sometimes the more famous a person is, the less need he has to specifically identify himself. For example, when one hears the name 'Elvis' there is no need to add 'the famous deceased rock star'. A similar thing could have been true of James. He was so well known due to his relationship with Jesus that he simply had no need of stating the relationship in the opening of his letter.

## What do we know about his life?

Having identified the author of this epistle, let's move on to the second question. What do we know about his life? Thankfully, the New Testament provides us with a great deal of information about the life of James.

The first place we encounter James the Lord's brother is when Jesus begins his teaching ministry in his hometown of Galilee. After hearing the authoritative teaching of Jesus in the synagogue, the crowd declares in astonishment, '"Isn't this the carpenter? Isn't this Mary's son *and the brother of James*, Joseph, Judas and Simon? Aren't his sisters here with us?" And they took offence at him' (Mark 6:3, emphasis mine). This text reveals that Jesus had a brother named James, and we know from John's Gospel that James did not immediately believe in Jesus: 'For even his own brothers did not believe in him' (John 7:5). The story of the life of James begins with his lack of faith.

Like the rest of Jesus' earthly family, James probably viewed Jesus as being 'out of his mind' (Mark 3:20-21). It is also very likely that he harboured some level of personal animosity towards Jesus. After all, it couldn't have been easy for James to grow up with a brother who was perfect in every way. Daniel Doriani compares James' relationship to Jesus to that of the Old Testament account of Joseph's relationship to his brothers: 'If, in Genesis 37, Joseph's brothers struggled with his sense that he was destined for greatness, imagine the difficulty of being Jesus' younger brother.'[6] Doriani even wonders whether James' parents might have corrected his behaviour by stating, 'Why can't you be more like Jesus?'[7] It is easy to see why James would be inclined to reject his brother. In fact, James' rejection of Jesus was so strong that James did not even attend his brother's execution. Only Jesus' mother is found at the cross; the rest of his family utterly rejected him.

So how did James become a believer? It is probable that James came to faith through the resurrection. In 1 Corinthians 15:7, Paul records the fact that Jesus revealed himself to James after the resurrection: 'Then *he appeared to James*, then to all the apostles' (emphasis mine). It is likely that this appearance triggered James' conversion.

After his conversion, James quickly ascended to a leadership position in the church. Peter testifies to James' leadership role as early as Acts 12:17 where he instructs the disciples in Mary's house to inform 'James and the brothers' about his miraculous release from Herod's prison. By setting apart the name 'James' from the other 'brothers', Peter tells us that James is a prominent figure in the Jerusalem church, worthy of being particularly named. Of course, the fact that James was a leader in the church is most clearly revealed in Acts 15, where he presides over the Jerusalem Council, gives a lengthy speech and suggests that a letter be sent to the churches setting out the council's decision (Acts 15:13-30). Other evidence for James' prominent role in the church can be gleaned from Paul's epistle to the Galatians, in which he refers to James as one of the 'pillars' of the church, thereby placing James in an illustrious class which included both Peter and John (Galatians 2:9). In fact, James' leadership role in the church of Jerusalem was so significant that most scholars agree that it is proper to refer to him as the first 'bishop' of Jerusalem.

## A pastor's heart

While James was indeed a high-powered church leader, we must be careful that this description does not lead us to embrace an erroneous picture of the man and his ministry. For example, thinking of James as a bishop may conjure up images of a church bureaucrat who is very distant from the people of the church. Such imagery is entirely at odds with who James was. Instead of conceiving of James as administrative bishop, we should see him primarily as a concerned and faithful pastor. The evidence for this portrait of James may be gleaned from his letter, which reveals his pastoral heart in two ways.

First, the epistle of James displays the pastoral heart of its author by means of its audience. In the opening verse, James describes his audience as 'the twelve tribes scattered among the nations' (James 1:1). While scholars debate the meaning of this reference, it seems most probable that it is addressing ethnic Jews who had converted to Christ and then were subsequently driven out of the Jerusalem church through the persecution which followed on the heels of the martyrdom of Stephen (Acts 8:1; and 11:19). In other words, James is most likely writing to former members of his Jerusalem flock who had lost everything as a result of their faith in Christ. Instead of writing them off, he writes *to* them. He extends the rod and staff of a determined and faithful shepherd. This letter is not a bureaucratic missive sent off to some powerful church, but rather it is a letter of pastoral challenge and encouragement written to people who have experienced persecution.

The second way that the epistle of James displays the pastoral heart of its author is by means of its genre. The epistle of James is really not an epistle at all, but rather, as most scholars readily acknowledge, it is a sermon or collection of sermons. James addresses the church not as a bureaucrat, but as a preacher. One cannot help but feel the pulse of a preacher's heart when reading this epistle. As J. A. Motyer has noted: 'As soon as we read through the letter of James we say to ourselves, "This man was a preacher before he was a writer."'[8]

Motyer cites the following evidence in support of the sermonic nature of this epistle:

1. James addresses his hearers 'directly' and 'pointedly' (e.g. 1:19-20);
2. James confronts, engages, exposes and corrects the erroneous thinking of his hearers (e.g. 4:13-14);
3. James keeps his hearers' attention by using 'startling statements' (e.g. 2:19), rhetorical questions (e.g. 2:14-16) and effective illustrations (e.g. 3:11-12);
4. James reveals his pastoral heart by identifying himself with his people, particularly by referring to them as 'brothers' (e.g. 1:2, 16, 19; 2:1, 5, 14; and 5:7, 9).[9]

James took the time to write to people who were outside of his direct realm of influence. He wrote to a church riddled with challenges such as divisiveness, favouritism, gossip, false teaching and materialism. He wrote to people who were hurting and who were at risk of totally misunderstanding the Christian life. He wrote to people who were in peril, both physically and spiritually. When he wrote to these scattered Jews, he wrote to them not as a distant church administrator, but rather as a pastor and a preacher. What the epistle of James tells us about the life of James is that he was a shepherd who cared for his flock.

## A man of piety

There is one final aspect to James' life which is worthy of our attention — his temperament and personal piety. Certainly, his temperament as a man is revealed in his epistle. As we have noted, he was a warmhearted and challenging pastor. However, we also see another aspect of James' temperament through the two accounts of his leadership decisions in the book of Acts. In both Acts 15 and Acts 21, James is called on to render judgement on a matter of conflict between Jews and Gentiles, particularly regarding whether Gentiles had to be circumcized. In both of these instances, the person seeking his counsel is the apostle Paul. James' judgement in these two matters displays that he was a man of wisdom and piety.

In Acts 15, at the Jerusalem Council, James supports Paul and declares that Gentiles need not be circumcized. But he also encourages the Gentiles to abstain from certain practices which would be offensive to the Jews, such as eating food offered to idols and eating meat from strangled animals (Acts 15:20).

In Acts 21:17-26, Paul again comes to Jerusalem to stand before James. This time there are rumours spreading that Paul is discouraging Jews from circumcizing their children. James responds by asking Paul to perform a ritual act in the temple to demonstrate to the Jews that he has respect for the law. Paul willingly submits to this request of James and follows through with the ritual. During this meeting, James also reaffirms his decision in Acts 15 that Gentiles need not be circumcized (Acts 21:21).

These two accounts reveal the balanced temperament of James. He was a man who promoted the peace of the church while ardently defending the truth of the gospel. In both Acts 15 and Acts 21, as the leading Jewish Christian in Jerusalem, James forcefully opposed legalism, and supported Paul by ruling that Gentiles need not be circumcized. But in both instances he also went to great lengths to avoid unnecessary offence to his fellow Jewish Christians. James was an even-tempered man. He was a skilful leader. He was a man of personal piety. The Puritan Thomas Manton provides the following description of James:

> Of so great temperance, that he drank neither wine nor strong drink, and ate no flesh. So pious, that his knees were made like a camel's hoof by frequent prayers.[10]

Because of his exemplary personal piety, temperance and service to the church, the church fathers frequently referred to James by the well-deserved title of 'James the Just'.

## A martyr

After serving Christ with his life as a pastor and pillar of the church, James was eventually martyred for the faith around A.D. 63. Thomas Manton, drawing on the work of the early church historian Eusebius, describes the martyrdom of James as follows:

> He died a martyr; they would have him persuade the people to abandon the doctrine of Christ, which, when he refused, and pressed the quite contrary, he was thrown down from a pinnacle of the temple, and his brains dashed out with a fuller's club, and so gave up the ghost.[11]

From an unbelieving brother of Jesus, to a leader of the church, to a passionate pastor, to a martyr for the faith — this is the story of the life of James. Having surveyed his life we now see how truly fitting the opening greeting of his epistle is: 'James, a servant of God and of the Lord Jesus Christ'. Having considered the unique aspects of the life of James, in the next chapter we'll explore some of the unique features of his letter.

# 2.

# James the letter

*'To the twelve tribes scattered among the nations: Greetings'*
(James 1:1).

In the previous chapter, I compared our journey through the epistle of James to a hike and noted that in order to have a successful hike we must have our backpacks filled with the right tools. One of the tools we need for a successful journey through James is a map. We need to have a grasp of the unique terrain of this letter so that we can stay on course as we journey through it. Accordingly, in this chapter we will take a quick flight over the epistle and note its unique features.

## A unique voice

When one reads the epistle of James, it simply sounds different from the other New Testament epistles. This difference can be explained partially by James' use of many unique words. For example, James uses 570 words in his epistle, and seventy-three of them occur nowhere else in the New Testament.[1] However, it is not just his vocabulary that provides a unique voice to this epistle. There are three additional factors.

First, James — more than any other New Testament epistle — speaks in the voice of Old Testament wisdom. In fact, James so mimics the voice of the Old Testament wisdom tradition that many scholars have compared it to the book of Proverbs.[2] While the epistle should not be equated with the Old Testament wisdom tradition[3], it is wholly appropriate to classify it as the only New Testament wisdom book. Like Proverbs, James speaks with a practical voice which applies the Word of God to real-life situations.

Second, the voice of James is also unique because it echoes with prophetic overtones. James not only mimics the sage of Proverbs by providing believers with wisdom, but he also imitates the probing voice of the prophets by calling God's people to repentance. As Dennis Johnson so aptly puts it: 'James sometimes sounds more like a fiery prophet than like a reflective observer of the way life works "under the sun".'[4] For example, note how James addresses the unrighteous rich in James 5:4-6:

> Look! The wages you failed to pay the workmen who mowed your fields are crying out against you. The cries of the harvesters have reached the ears of the Lord Almighty. You have lived on earth in luxury and self-indulgence. You have fattened yourselves in the day of slaughter. You have condemned and murdered innocent men, who were not opposing you.

These words seem as if they were lifted directly from the lips of prophets like Amos, Micah or Zephaniah.[5] With the force of an Old Testament prophet, James issues a warning regarding the horrific reality of the coming day of the Lord.

A third characteristic that distinguishes James' voice is that, more so than any other New Testament book, it emphasizes faith in action. For example, there are over fifty commands in the 108 verses of the epistle of James. The letter also employs imperative verbs (verbs which demand action) more frequently than any other New Testament book.[6] James speaks with an active voice calling his hearers to apply the Word of God to real life.

## A unique message

In addition to exhibiting a unique voice, the epistle of James is also unique in regard to its main message. This is because it places such extraordinary emphasis on the practical aspects of Christian living. We can see this in both the structure and content of the epistle.

While all the New Testament epistles contain some practical application, they also contain significant doctrinal sections. For example, consider the Pauline epistles. Paul frequently begins his letters with doctrine and then concludes them with practical application. This customary pattern can be seen in Paul's letter to the Ephesians in which he spends the first three chapters providing deep doctrinal insights and then uses the remaining three chapters to apply this doctrine to the Christian life.

What makes James unique is that his entire epistle is much like the second half of most of Paul's epistles. Throughout his epistle James touches upon such practical matters as dealing with trials and temptations, the need for wisdom, dealing with wealth and poverty, responding to the Word of God, avoiding partiality, evidencing our faith through deeds, controlling our speech and our passions, preventing pride, the power of prayer and the need to correct our fellow believers. From beginning to end, the epistle of James explores various aspects of the Christian life. It focuses almost entirely on the practical outworking of the Christian life and is almost entirely void of the extended theological discourses that we are so accustomed to when encountering Paul's letters.

While James does not provide us with theological discourses like Paul, this does not mean that James is not 'theological'. Rather, the lack of such discourses simply demonstrates that his purpose is entirely focused on the practical aspects of the Christian life. James did not include deep theological discourses because he presupposed that his hearers knew and accepted the theology of Christ. James' purpose is to encourage those who have accepted the theology of Christ to adopt in practice the life of Christ. His purpose is pastoral. He is writing to encourage and admonish Christians to live like Christians. James assumes belief, but demands action. We see this purpose revealed in James 2:18-20:

> But someone will say, 'You have faith; I have deeds.' Show me your faith without deeds, and I will show you my faith by what I do. You believe that there is one God. Good! Even the demons believe that — and shudder. You foolish man, do you want evidence that faith without deeds is useless?

James does not hide his intentions. His purpose is to call professing Christians to put their faith to work, to put their faith to the test.

As you can see, the unique voice and message of this epistle make it well suited to serve as a summary guide for the Christian life. In James we have the voice of Jesus continuing through apostolic authority and speaking directly to the issues of life in the Christian church. In James we find the voice of Jesus once again calling us to pick up our cross and follow him. In James we are reminded that professing Jesus with our lips is not enough — we must live like Jesus as well. Do you see how relevant this message is for our own day? If there is anything that is crippling the power of the church in our day it is Christians who hear the Word but fail to live the Word. As D. Edmond Hiebert notes, 'As long as there are professed Christians who are prone to separate profession and practice, the message of this epistle will continue to be relevant.'[7] It is this continual divorce between faith professed and faith practised which makes the epistle of James so timeless and so necessary today.

## Uniquely Christ-centred

One of the criticisms levelled against the epistle of James is that it lacks a sufficient focus on Jesus Christ and the essence of the Christian gospel. It is true that there are scant explicit references to Jesus in the epistle. Jesus' name only appears twice in the entire letter. It is also true that James does not mention significant redemptive events like the death, resurrection and ascension of Jesus Christ. Factors such as these have led some scholars to view James as 'sub-Christian'. One prominent New Testament scholar has referred to the epistle of James as 'the most Jewish, the most undistinctively Christian document in the New Testament'.[8] Are the critics correct in their assessment of the epistle of James? Is James indeed a sub-Christian document devoid of any connections to Christ? Absolutely not! The epistle of James is intensely Christ-centred, but the way James speaks of Jesus is very different from all the other New Testament writers. James is uniquely Christ-centred. He speaks of Jesus in three ways.

The first way James speaks of Jesus is by speaking in the voice of wisdom. We've already noted that one of the distinctive aspects of the epistle of James is its similarity to the Old Testament wisdom tradition. Biblical wisdom does not occur in a vacuum, but rather it always occurs in the context of God's covenant relationship with his people. Jesus is the mediator of that covenant. In other words, Jesus is the one who gives wisdom to us. However, Jesus not only dispenses wisdom, but he is the very source of all wisdom as Paul clearly points out in his letter to the Colossians:

> My purpose is that they may be encouraged in heart and united in love, so that they may have the full riches of complete understanding, in order that they may know the mystery of God, namely, Christ, in whom are hidden all the treasures of wisdom and knowledge
>
> (Colossians 2:2-3).

James is an epistle of wisdom, and whenever we encounter wisdom in the Bible we also encounter Jesus Christ, the giver and source of wisdom.

Secondly, James also speaks of Jesus by means of the eschatological emphasis of his epistle. In theology, eschatology is the study of what will happen after the end of the age in which we presently live. James emphasizes eschatology by frequently reminding his readers of the reality that this age will indeed come to an end. He emphasizes this truth in order to comfort and challenge his readers. For instance, he comforts those who suffer in this present age by reminding them of the joys they will experience in the age to come. On the other hand, he also sternly warns those who are living contrary to God's commands by reminding them of the coming judgement which will be meted out in the Day of the Lord. James tells us that in order to faithfully live the Christian life we must appropriate into this present age the realities of Christ's return and the age to come. The reality of the impending return of Jesus Christ is the indicative which fuels all of James' imperatives. In this sense, every verse of this epistle is Christ-centred.

The third, and perhaps most powerful, way we encounter Jesus in James is through the echoes of our Lord's voice which resound throughout this epistle. No other New Testament epistle captures the voice of Jesus like the epistle of James. The voice of Jesus is manifested in this epistle in a variety of ways. Sometimes it is made apparent through near-verbatim quotations. For example, consider the following comparison between James 5:12 and Matthew 5:33-37:

| James 5:12 | Matthew 5:33-37 |
|---|---|
| Above all, my brothers, *do not swear — not by heaven or by earth* or by anything else. Let your *'Yes' be yes, and your 'No,' no,* or you will be condemned. | Again, you have heard that it was said to the people long ago, 'Do not break your oath, but keep the oaths you have made to the Lord.' But I tell you, *Do not swear at all: either by heaven,* for it is God's throne; or by the earth, for it is his footstool; or by Jerusalem, for it is the city of the Great King. And *do not swear* by your head, for you cannot make even one hair white or black. *Simply let your 'Yes' be 'Yes,' and your 'No,' 'No';* anything beyond this comes from the evil one. |

In addition to direct quotations, James also embodies the voice of Jesus in his epistle through frequent allusions to Jesus' teaching. These allusions are so significant that some scholars have concluded that the entire epistle is an extended homily on Jesus' Sermon on the Mount.[9] While other New Testament epistles quote from and allude to the teachings of Jesus, none speak so fluently in the voice of Jesus as does the epistle of

James. Biblical scholar Douglas Moo notes that James 'weaves Jesus' teaching into the very fabric of his own instruction'.[10] Another scholar, Luke Timothy Johnson, comments that James naturally uses 'his brother's language as his own'.[11] When one reads the epistle of James one encounters, in a unique way, the voice of Jesus speaking to the life of the church and the life of the Christian.

## The journey begins

Now that we have become acquainted with James the man and James the letter, it is time for us to begin our journey. It is time for us to rediscover the riches of the long-neglected treasures which are buried in the epistle of James. But in order to rediscover its riches you must be willing to embark on a challenging journey that will test your faith.

Committing to a journey through James is like committing to a physical exercise programme with James serving as your personal trainer — except James is not trying to increase the size of your biceps, but rather the size of your faith. As such, he will not let you take the easy way out. He will not let your faith experience atrophy, in which the muscles in our body degenerate when we fail to use them, so that they become smaller and weaker. James will *never* allow this to happen to your faith because he will constantly press you to extend your limits and to reach new heights of spiritual development. Here is just a sample of the penetrating challenges found in his letter:

James 1:22: 'Do not merely listen to the word, and so deceive yourselves. Do what it says.'

James 2:10: 'For whoever keeps the whole law and yet stumbles at just one point is guilty of breaking all of it.'

James 3:13: 'Who is wise and understanding among you? Let him show it by his good life, by deeds done in the humility that comes from wisdom.'

James 4:4: 'You adulterous people, don't you know that friendship with the world is hatred towards God? Anyone who chooses to be a friend of the world becomes an enemy of God.'

James 5:9: 'Don't grumble against each other, brothers, or you will be judged. The Judge is standing at the door!'

As you can see from this sample, James will indeed challenge you. As one commentator put it: 'Ask James, "Does the road wind up-hill all the way?" and hear him reply, "Yes, to the very end."'[12]

When you journey into the epistle of James you enter into the gymnasium of faith. Like the Sermon on the Mount, the epistle of James calls us to live the kingdom ethic which was established and exemplified by Christ our Saviour. Like Jesus, James sets the bar high. The good news is that by setting the bar so high James reminds us that we cannot measure up to this standard in our own strength. This is how James most clearly speaks of Jesus. By constantly challenging us with the high standards of the Christian life, James cleverly exposes our desperate need of Jesus. He reminds us that the Christian life can only be lived through our enlivening union with Christ. James experienced this power of Christ in his own life, and he wants his readers — he wants you — to experience it as well. Are you ready to begin the journey? Are you prepared for the workout? Are you ready to have your faith tested? Are you ready to embrace the challenge that is the Christian life?

# 3.

# The reasons for our trials

*'Consider it pure joy, my brothers, whenever you face trials of many kinds, because you know that the testing of your faith develops perseverance. Perseverance must finish its work so that you may be mature and complete, not lacking anything'*
(James 1:2-4).

One Sunday morning, after the worship service, a young woman approached me and asked if we could get together to talk. I agreed to her request, and we arranged a breakfast meeting at a local restaurant. Through my pastoral experience, I have come to realize that when people want to talk with me it is usually not for the purpose of sharing good news, and this was certainly the case with this young woman. Even though I went into that meeting prepared to hear about a trial, I was still overwhelmed by what this young woman shared with me. She shared a detailed account of her father's debilitating heart illness and how many times he had been near death. She recounted to me the numerous surgeries and the vast array of medications which were necessary to preserve her father's life. She also explained to me the incredible stress and strains experienced by her family as a result of her father's illness.

At this point in our conversation I was already overwhelmed by her trial, but there was more. She proceeded to share with me that she had recently been diagnosed with the same congenital heart condition as her father. I found myself staring into the tear-filled eyes of a woman in her twenties who was now facing a lifetime of physical and emotional challenges. Of course, the natural question on her mind was, '*Why?*' Why did she and her father have to endure such trials? This is a very appropriate question to ask. It is also a question that I, as a pastor, should have anticipated and been prepared to answer. On that particular morning, however, I felt utterly unable to answer this question. I simply listened and prayed with her.

My initial response to this woman's trial was not wrong. It is often wise to initially respond to the trials of others with a listening ear and a sympathetic heart rather than reacting immediately with deep theological thoughts. The most helpful response of Job's incompetent comforters was their initial willingness to sit in silence with Job for seven days (Job 2:13). After an appropriate period of empathizing, however, it is important to address the question, 'Why?' This question cannot be left unanswered, because a failure to address it ultimately trivializes a person's suffering and can even lead them to doubt their faith.

Perhaps you are presently enduring a trial. Perhaps you feel lonely or depressed. Perhaps you are dealing with what seems like an unsolvable problem or irreconcilable conflict. Perhaps you have lost your job or someone you loved. Perhaps you are battling a chronic disease. In the midst of trials such as these we often appropriately ask 'Why?' It is likely that the Jewish Christians to whom James was writing were asking similar questions.

James was writing to people who had experienced trials. The book of Acts reveals that after the stoning of Stephen the church in Jerusalem faced 'great persecution' which forced many of the

Christians to flee Jerusalem (Acts 8:1-4). Acts also informs us that some of the Christians affected by this persecution were scattered as far as 'Phoenicia, Cyprus and Antioch' (Acts 11:19). It is likely that James wrote his epistle to these dispersed and persecuted Jewish Christians, so he was preaching to people who had lost nearly everything due to their faith. Believing in Jesus had seemingly brought nothing but trials into their lives. They had lost their homes and jobs. They were forced to relocate and faced personal peril in the form of persecution. Given this reality, it is not surprising that the first issue James tackles in his letter is that of trials. James opens his epistle by answering the 'Why?' question. He provides us with three reasons why God sends trials into our lives.

## To test our faith

According to James, the first reason we encounter trials is to test our faith. James explicitly states this reason in the third verse of his epistle where, after mentioning the inevitability of trials, he reveals that these trials are for the 'testing of your faith'. What does this phrase mean?

The Greek word which is translated as 'testing' (*dokimion*) in James 1:3 is used twice in the Greek version of the Old Testament, the version which was most likely used by James. Note how both occurrences of this word suggest that what James has in mind is the Old Testament imagery of the refiner's fire:

Psalm 12:6:      'And the words of the LORD are flawless, like silver *refined* (*dokimion*) in a furnace of clay, purified seven times.'

Proverbs 27:21:  'The crucible for silver and the furnace for gold, but man is *tested* (*dokimion*) by the praise he receives.'

The apostle Peter, the only other New Testament writer who employs this word, uses it in a similar way to the Old Testament texts cited above: 'These have come so that your faith — of greater worth than gold, which perishes even though *refined* (*dokimion*) by fire — may be proved genuine and may result in praise, glory and honour when Jesus Christ is revealed' (1 Peter 1:7). James tells us that one of the reasons God places trials in our lives is to put our faith to the test in order to determine its genuineness. God uses trials as a means of revealing the depth of our allegiance to him. Just as the furnace is useful in testing the fortitude and purity of metal, God uses trials to test our spiritual mettle.

Doesn't your own experience confirm that trials are an effective means of testing the strength and sincerity of our faith? If you are like me, you know of people who, after enduring a difficult trial, have rejected the faith. Again, if you are like me, you know of people who have been immersed in a sea of great trials only to emerge even stronger in their faith. Trials are an effective means of testing our faith because it is in the midst of trials that we often reveal what we truly believe about God. As J. A. Motyer notes, 'When circumstances seem to mock our creed, when the cruelty of life denies his fatherliness, his silence calls in question his almightiness and the sheer, haphazard, meaningless jumble of events challenges the possibility of a Creator's ordering hand. It is in this way that life's trials test our faith for genuineness.'[1] One of the reasons God sends trials into our lives is to test our faith.

## To cultivate perseverance in us

James informs us that a second reason why we endure trials is to cultivate perseverance in us. James reveals this reason at the end of verse three: 'the testing of your faith *develops perseverance*' (emphasis mine). The first thing which is implicitly revealed in this verse is that James assumes that Christians will successfully pass the testing of their faith through trials. Don't miss the significance of this presumption. James assumes that when our faith is tested by trials we will prevail and move on to develop perseverance. When God tests our faith with a trial, his purpose is not to produce failure in us, but rather to produce perseverance in us. Even our seeming human failures during trials are used by God to cultivate our perseverance. This should bring great encouragement to us in the midst of our trials.

So what does James mean by perseverance? The Greek word which is translated as 'perseverance' is the word '*hypomone*', which could also be translated as 'steadfastness', 'endurance' or 'fortitude'. Douglas Moo defines *hypomone* by suggesting the following image: 'The picture is of a person successfully carrying a heavy load for a long time.'[2] This image describes the state of many people who have endured trials in the congregations I have served. It makes me think of the woman who has battled lung cancer for over a decade. She has carried a heavy load for a long time. It makes me think of her husband who has sacrificially cared for her during her illness. He too has carried a heavy load for a long time. The image makes me think of the man who lost both his wife and daughter to tragic accidents. He has carried a heavy load for a long time. Perhaps you have also carried a heavy load for a long time. How does such a burden cultivate perseverance in us? Let me suggest two ways.

First, carrying the weight of our trials cultivates perseverance in us by making us stronger. One of the ways long-distance runners train for a marathon is by wearing ankle weights. They train with these weights for months in advance of the marathon, forcing themselves to carry the additional burden in order to strengthen their leg muscles and build their endurance. As a result, when the time comes to actually run the race they can run farther and faster. The heavy load of our trials strengthens us in a similar fashion. Trials build the muscle of our faith and enable us to run with greater endurance the marathon that is the Christian life.

Second, carrying the weight of our trials cultivates perseverance in us by forcing us to rely more and more on the grace of God. The apostle Paul immediately comes to mind here. Paul carried a heavy load for a long time through his chronic ailment which he referred to as a 'thorn in my flesh' (2 Corinthians 12:7). He prayed fervently for this burden to be lifted, but God did not remove it. Instead God explained to Paul that carrying this heavy load was a way of reminding him of his need of God's grace. God answered Paul's prayers with these words: 'My grace is sufficient for you, for my power is made perfect in weakness' (2 Corinthians 12:9).

The heavy load of trials cultivates perseverance in us by making us stronger and forcing us to rely on the true source of our perseverance — the grace of God. One of the reasons God sends trials into our lives is to cultivate perseverance in us.

## To bring us to perfection

The third and final reason for our trials, according to James, is to bring us to perfection. James sets forth this reason in verse four: 'Perseverance must finish its work so that you *may be mature and complete, not lacking anything*' (emphasis mine). Through this triad ('mature', 'complete' and 'not lacking anything') James draws for us a composite picture of perfection. Each component of this triad, and even the word 'finish', could arguably be translated as 'perfect'. Thus, James 1:4 could be loosely translated as follows: 'Perseverance must *perfect* its work so that you may be *perfect, perfect and perfect*.' Through this unmistakable emphasis on perfection James reveals to us the ultimate reason why God allows us to suffer trials — to make us perfect.

How does God do this? Again, let me give you an example from my own pastoral experience. At one of the churches I have served we ordained two deacons during a Sunday evening service. One of these deacons makes his living as a contractor. His ordination to the office of deacon was a significant event for him. He was excited about beginning to serve God in the ministry of mercy. On the Sunday evening of his ordination, he was at a spiritual high point in his life. Little did he know that things were about to change drastically. The very next day this deacon was working on a roofing job. As he stepped off the roof, his ladder gave way under his feet and he came crashing down to the pavement below. His wife, who works with him, was able to help him into their truck, and they rushed off to the emergency department of the hospital. Our new deacon soon learned that he had four broken ribs and a punctured lung. He also learned that he would not be able to work for six to eight weeks. Not only did he find himself in incredible pain, but he also found himself wondering how he would provide for his wife and five young children. On his first day as a minister of mercy, he found himself in desperate need of mercy. He found himself in a trial.

Of course, almost immediately the congregation responded to his needs. The deacons extended financial support, as did many individuals, as well. There was an outpouring of support for him and his family. After experiencing this expression of mercy, he commented to me that his trial had made him a better deacon because it forced him to take the perspective of an individual in need. The experience of becoming needy helped him to become more sensitive to other people's needs. His trial was formative in building his character. This is an example of how trials are used by God to perfect us — they build our character. Trials serve to remove our sinful traits *from* us, and they also serve to spawn and strengthen godly traits *in* us.

This emphasis on the character-building power of trials is at the heart of James' triad ('mature and complete, not lacking anything'). This triad implies a progressive and incremental process by which we are shaped into well-rounded Christians. For example, Peter Davids suggests the following definition of James' concept of perfection: 'Perfection is not just a maturing of character, but a rounding out as more and more "parts" of the righteous character are added.'[3] Trials help us to become perfect, to become more righteous in every aspect of our lives. Trials are like a sculpting knife in the hands of God. He uses them to smooth our rough edges and to transform us into the glorious, and perfect, image of his Son. The ultimate reason why God sends trials into our lives is to bring us to perfection.

## The chain of Christian maturity

James informs us that trials are used by God to test our faith, to cultivate perseverance in us and to bring us to perfection. It is crucial to grasp that James does not view these three reasons as unrelated to each other but rather as conjoined links which form a chain of Christian maturity. According to James, God uses trials to set in motion a chain reaction in our lives. Trials first test the sincerity and genuineness of our faith. This testing, and proving, of our faith then serves to cultivate perseverance in us. This perseverance, in turn, develops within us the perfect character of Christ. Simply put, James tells us that the fire of our trials ultimately leads us to becoming stronger Christians. This is why, according to James, God sends trials into our lives. Let me illustrate James' point.

Presently, I live in western Pennsylvania, near the city of Pittsburgh. There was a time when Pittsburgh was known as the steel capital of the world. Steel is an incredibly strong and long-lasting metal. But it can be made even stronger and more enduring through a process known as tempering. Tempering involves repeatedly heating metal alloy to a near-critical temperature and then immediately cooling it back to room temperature. Heating the metal alloy to high temperatures removes certain unwanted properties present in the metal, and the rapid cooling process prevents those unwanted properties from being reabsorbed into the metal. This process puts the metal alloy under tremendous stress, but the end result of this process is an incredibly strong type of steel known as 'tempered steel'.

Pastor James tells us that the Christian life is a tempering process. God places our lives in the fire of trials in order to make us 'mature and complete, not lacking anything'. James teaches us that God often places us in the heat of trials to expose and remove our sinfulness. Each time we suffer a trial we emerge from the heat even stronger, like tempered steel. The pathway to perfection in the Christian life is paved with trials.

## Perfect through suffering

Now I realize that James' brutal honesty about the role of trials in our lives may not immediately strike you as all that comforting. One could conclude that what James is saying here is no more than the popular slogan 'No pain, no gain.' That's not very comforting to someone enduring trials.

Thankfully, that is not what James is saying here. When James tells us that our trials are meant to make us perfect, what he is doing is drawing back the curtains of heaven to show us the ultimate divine purpose of trials. This provides us with hope in the here and now. Nothing provides an exhausted marathon runner with a fresh jolt of adrenaline like the sight of the finish line. By setting before us our perfect glorification in the age to come, James essentially shows us the finish line of our faith. He does this to encourage us.

There's one more thing James is showing us here. By telling us that our trials are being used to perfect us, James is also revealing to us the comforting truth that our lives as Christians are patterned after the life of our Lord. The author to the Hebrews informs us that Jesus was made 'perfect through suffering' (Hebrews 2:10). Jesus endured great trials so that he could become our great High Priest. Because Jesus was perfected for this office by means of his own suffering, he is now able not only to sympathize with us in our trials, but, more importantly, he is able to provide us with grace in our time of need (Hebrews 4:16). Therefore, whenever you find yourself in trials of many kinds, be encouraged by the knowledge that the one who was made perfect through his suffering is the one who is perfecting you through your trials.

# 4.

# Responding to our trials

*'Consider it pure joy, my brothers,*
*whenever you face trials of many kinds'*
(James 1:2).

◆ ◆ ◆

*'Be patient, then, brothers, until the Lord's coming. See how*
*the farmer waits for the land to yield its valuable crop and*
*how patient he is for the autumn and spring rains. You too,*
*be patient and stand firm, because the Lord's coming is near'*
(James 5:7-8).

A popular cultural proverb states, 'When life gives you lemons, make lemonade.' The point of the proverb is that when trials come into our lives we should respond to them by simply making the most of them. Across the ages, from the emotionless stiff upper lip of the stoics to the 'Pollyannaish' view of modern self-help gurus, humanity has continually attempted to provide an answer to the question of how we should respond to trials and suffering. When it comes to encountering trials we not only want to know *why* we encounter them, but we also want to know *how* to properly respond to them.

In the previous chapter, we explored James' answer to the 'Why?' question. We learned that God sends trials into our lives to test our faith, cultivate perseverance in us and bring us to perfection. In this chapter we'll explore James' answer to the 'How?' question. We'll see that James teaches us that we should respond to our trials in two ways — with joy and with patience.

## Joy

As a preacher, I have come to recognize how helpful it is to start a sermon with an attention-grabbing introduction. Most modern preaching books agree that this technique is helpful, and they suggest a variety of ways to achieve this goal. One of the best ways to grab the attention of your hearers is to make a shocking statement which catches your audience off guard. This is exactly what James did at the beginning of his sermon on trials. He introduces his sermon with these words: '*Consider it pure joy*, my brothers, whenever you face trials of many kinds' (James 1:2, emphasis mine).

Consider it pure joy? Think about that opening for a moment and its impact on its original hearers. James' original audience consisted of people who had suffered greatly for their faith. They had endured physical, economic and social trials. Imagine this audience of weary pilgrims eagerly gathered together to hear words of comfort and consolation from their pastor, and instead they receive a call to consider their trials as pure joy. This unexpected imperative would certainly have grabbed their attention!

When one examines James' command to 'consider it pure joy' on a deeper level it becomes even more shocking. The Greek word which is translated as 'consider' means to render a deliberate cognitive judgement about something. James told his readers that they must resolve in their minds that their trials, no matter how physically painful and unpleasant, were ultimately spiritually joyful. In addition, James' use of the adjective 'pure' to modify the noun 'joy' only serves to add to the stunning nature of his imperative. The word 'pure' is actually a translation of the Greek word for 'all'. By placing the word 'all' before the word 'joy' James is emphasizing that Christians must consider their trials as wholly, completely, entirely and utterly joyful. James told his readers that they should not have even a drop of sadness mixed in their libation of joy. Clearly, this is a shocking and radical command.

We need to proceed with great caution here, because it is very easy to misinterpret this opening statement of James. For instance, one could interpret this imperative as a call to take perverse pleasure in our own suffering. This is not the meaning of James' imperative. He is not calling us to actually celebrate or revel in our trials. As R. Kent Hughes notes, 'James was not commending that we exult upon hearing that our career position has been given to our secretary, or that the neighbor's children have leukemia, or that one's spouse is adulterous.'[1] Alternatively, one could interpret this imperative as a perverse call to actively seek out trials as a means to acquire greater joy, to conclude that where trials abound, joy abounds all the more. Again, this would represent a gross misreading of the text. James is not suggesting that we engage in some type of monastic self-flagellation through which we attempt to seek trials as a pathway to experiencing earthly joy. Both of these misinterpretations entirely miss James' point. However, if these interpretations are incorrect, then what exactly did James mean by his shocking statement?

When James calls us to consider our trials as pure joy, he is calling us to make a spiritual judgement regarding our circum-stances. James wants us to foster an inner heart attitude of joy. This joy is a state of mind which can only be achieved when we view our present trials in the light of eternal realities. What James is demanding is that we place our present trials on one side of a balance scale and weigh them against the glories of the age to come. He is admonishing us to understand our lives in retrospect from the standpoint of our glorification. In other words, if our lives were a novel, James would instruct us to read it in reverse order. He would tell us to begin reading our lives from the end of our story and then work our way back to our present circumstances. By reading our lives in this way, we can have joy because we know that no matter how painful our present circumstances, our life story ultimately has a glorious ending in Jesus Christ. Thus, James is not calling us to perversely seek out trials or to deny the real pain we are experiencing, but rather he is calling us to adopt the mindset of the apostle Paul expressed in Romans 8:18: 'I consider that *our present sufferings* are not worth comparing *with the glory that will be revealed in us*' (emphasis mine).[2]

James informs us that as Christians we are able to have joy in the midst of trials because we are fully aware that God is the author of our trials and that he is using them for our ultimate good (Romans 8:28). The tears of our trials are part of the divine ink God uses to write the glorious redemptive story of our lives. Our trials are evidence that he is working on us in his heavenly workshop.

Once we accept this reality, we are enabled to respond to even the most dreadful circumstances with an inner attitude of peaceful joy, knowing that our loving Father is at work in our lives. John Calvin expressed it this way in his commentary on James:

> We certainly dread diseases, and want, and exile, and prison, and reproach, and death, because we regard them as evils; but when we understand that they are turned through God's kindness unto helps and aids to our salvation, it is ingratitude to murmur, and not willingly to submit to be thus paternally dealt with.[3]

As we saw in the previous chapter, God uses our trials to prove our faith, to cultivate perseverance in us and to perfect us. Accordingly, when Christians endure trials they understand that their trials are not the result of random and arbitrary acts of the universe, but rather as evidence of God's fatherly love in our lives. God is using our earthly trials to make us ready for our heavenly home. This is why we can make a deliberate judgement, through the gift of faith, to consider our present trials as pure joy.

By calling us to respond to our trials in this manner, James is once again echoing the words of his brother Jesus: 'Blessed are you when *people insult you, persecute you and falsely say all kinds of evil* against you because of me. *Rejoice and be glad, because great is your reward in heaven*' (Matthew 5:11-12, emphasis mine). James, like Jesus, calls us to respond to our trials with joy because great is our reward in heaven! This is the mindset that James is calling for in his shocking opening imperative.

## Patience

One of the structural patterns of this letter is that James often introduces a major topic in the first chapter of his epistle and then expounds on that very same theme, in greater detail, later on in the epistle. James does this with the topic of how to respond to trials. In the final chapter of his epistle, in James 5:7-11, he once again returns to this subject. In this section of his epistle, he reveals to us the second way we should respond to our trials. He calls us to respond to our trials with patience. Note how James emphasizes patience in the first two verses of this section, 'Be *patient*, then, brothers, until the Lord's coming. See how the farmer *waits* for the land to yield its valuable crop and how *patient* he is for the autumn and spring rains. You too, be *patient* and stand firm, because the Lord's coming is near,' (emphasis mine). Clearly, James is calling us to respond to our trials with patience.

This second response to our trials is as equally challenging as the first. After all, when we encounter a trial our natural response is to do everything we can to bring it to an immediate end. Given this reaction, we often become frustrated, angry and impatient with God when our trials continue for extended periods of time. It was likely that the people to whom James was writing were experiencing this natural type of impatience due to their own enduring trials. Like the psalmist in the midst of his trials, and like us in the midst of our trials, the people to whom James was writing were probably wondering, 'How long, O LORD?' (Psalm 6:3).

James, as a good pastor, recognized that his flock was struggling with this issue, and so he told them how to respond to extended trials. However, note that he did not offer them a 'quick fix'. He did not promise them that there was a light at the end of the tunnel. He offered no hollow platitudes of comfort. He did not even pretend to know how long their trials would last. Rather, he simply told them to 'Be patient' (James 5:7), to respond to their trials with patient perseverance.

After issuing this command to be patient, James proceeded to give his flock two illustrations to help them understand and apply this imperative. The first illustration was drawn from the agricultural world in which he lived. The second illustration was drawn from the Old Testament. James told his congregation about the patient farmer and the patient patriarch.

## The patient farmer

We live in an age in which we expect instantaneous results. We microwave our food in minutes, go on diets and exercise programmes which promise us a total body makeover in a matter of weeks, and we have a plethora of information instantly accessible at our fingertips through the Internet — all we have to do is just 'point and click'. We live in an impatient age. Farmers, however, are required to be patient. Even with the technological advances which have come to the world of agriculture, farmers must still plant and wait patiently for a harvest. James draws upon this imagery to illustrate our need to be patient in the face of trials: 'Be patient, then, brothers, until the Lord's coming. *See how the farmer waits for the land to yield its valuable crop and how patient he is for the autumn and spring rains.* You too, be patient and stand firm, because the Lord's coming is near' (James 5:7-8, emphasis mine).

Farmers in the ancient Near East, much like farmers today, were dependent on the weather for a good harvest. They had to wait patiently for rain. First came the 'autumn', or 'early', rains which served to germinate newly planted seeds. Next were the heavy rains of the winter season which helped these seeds grow into young plants. Finally, there were the 'spring' rains of April and May, which served to bring the crop to full harvestable maturity. An ancient Near Eastern farmer was entirely dependent on this weather cycle. He was forced to wait patiently for the rain and for his harvest.

James uses the example of the patient farmer to illustrate to us our need to be patient in our trials. Our trials are like a seed which, given time, will produce a spiritual harvest. What is the spiritual harvest produced by our trials? The spiritual harvest James refers to here is the chain of maturity he outlined in James 1:2-4. He is once again reminding us that trials are used by God to test our faith, cultivate perseverance in us and conform us to the perfect image of Christ. When will this great harvest occur? Again, James reminds us to take an eternal and heavenly perspective. He tells us that the harvest will not be complete 'until the Lord's coming' (James 5:7). Therefore, James calls us to respond to our trials like the patient farmer. We too must wait for the harvest. James is speaking directly to us when he declares, 'You too, be patient and stand firm, because the Lord's coming is near' (James 5:8).

James honestly informs us that some of our trials will have no satisfactory resolution in this life. Some of our trials will not end until *the* end, that is, until the end of the age. James responds to the psalmist's question — 'How long, O LORD?' — with the following answer: 'until the Lord's coming' (James 5:7). He calls us to be as patient as a farmer in the midst of trials. We are called to wait patiently like a farmer for the harvest at the coming of the Lord.

## The patient patriarch

James also draws on the Old Testament to illustrate his command to display patience in the face of trials. He first uses the example of the prophets: 'Brothers, as an example of patience in the face of suffering, take the prophets who spoke in the name of the Lord. As you know, we consider blessed those who have persevered' (James 5:10-11). The prophets patiently preached the same faithful message even as they were persecuted, rejected and ignored. They are exemplars of patience in the face of trials.

After referring to the prophets in general, James then gives his flock a specific example of an Old Testament figure who displayed patience in the face of trials. 'You have heard of Job's perseverance and have seen what the Lord finally brought about,' James writes. 'The Lord is full of compassion and mercy' (James 5:11). James calls us to consider God's servant Job. He calls us to consider the patient patriarch.

James' choice of Job is an obvious one. After all, Job was a man who endured great trials and testing. Like James' flock, Job too had suffered personally, physically, socially and economically as a direct result of his relationship with God. Job had lost his children through the persecutions of Satan. He endured physical afflictions in his body. He was socially ostracized by the insinuation of his 'comforters' that his suffering was a result of his sin. He was impoverished by the destruction of his home and crops. Job suffered much. He understood the nature of trials.

So how did Job respond to his trials? He responded in a variety of ways. At first, he was actually quite impatient about them. He actively questioned God about the difficulties he was enduring. Job was not a superhero; he too was human. However, when we consider the entire account of Job's ordeal we soon realize that he patiently endured his trials and remained steadfast in his faith.

Douglas Moo writes: 'Although Job did complain bitterly about God's treatment of him, he never abandoned his faith. In the midst of his incomprehension, he clung to God and continued to hope in him (see 1:21; 2:10; 16:19-21; 19:25-27).'[4] Job was patient in the midst of trials, and the conclusion of the book of Job reveals that his patience was richly rewarded. For everything Job lost he received back double from God. Consider the following verses from the end of the book of Job:

The LORD blessed the latter part of Job's life more than the first. He had fourteen thousand sheep, six thousand camels, a thousand yoke of oxen and a thousand donkeys. And he also had seven sons and three daughters ... Nowhere in all the land were there found women as beautiful as Job's daughters, and their father granted them an inheritance along with their brothers. After this, Job lived a hundred and forty years; he saw his children and their children to the fourth generation. And so he died, old and full of years

(Job 42:12-13, 15-17).

It is this part of Job's story that James calls his people to remember when he states in verse 11 that they 'have seen what the Lord finally brought about'. James called his congregation to read the novel of Job's life in reverse order. He called them to read from the end of the story and work their way back. When Job's life is read in this manner we see that, like the farmer who patiently awaits his harvest, Job patiently endured his trials and was rewarded in the end. Job discovered, as James notes, that 'The Lord is full of compassion and mercy' (5:11).

James tells us that if we emulate the patience of Job in the midst of our trials, then we too will be richly rewarded in the age to come. Like Job, we will experience the abundant compassion and mercy of the Lord. If we are patient, one day everything will be set right.

## For the joy set before him

When trials come into our lives we often respond to them with panic, anxiety, frustration, fear or anger. These are the normal human responses to trials. James, however, is *not* calling us to live like normal humans; rather, he is calling us to live like Christians who are 'mature and complete, not lacking anything' (James 1:4). James calls us as Christians to respond to our trials with an eternally motivated joy that yields present-day patience.

By issuing this call to us, James is once again urging us to imitate our Lord. Jesus endured the trials of his earthly life with godly joy and patience. He joyfully and patiently endured the humiliation of being 'born of a woman' and 'born under law' (Galatians 4:4). He joyfully and patiently endured the persecutions of men. He joyfully and patiently endured these trials because he understood the eternal ramifications and rewards of his suffering. He knew that a bountiful harvest was coming. Because of this eternal perspective, Jesus was able — *'for the joy set before him'* — to endure the greatest trial of all, the agony of the cross, scorning its shame (Hebrews 12:2, emphasis mine). And after enduring this trial Jesus received his reward as he 'sat down at the right hand of the throne of God' (12:2). James reminds us that when we are in the throes of our trials we can be encouraged because we are being conformed to the image of Christ.

# 5.
# Wisdom and the Christian life
# – Part 1

*'If any of you lacks wisdom, he should ask God, who gives generously to all without finding fault, and it will be given to him. But when he asks, he must believe and not doubt, because he who doubts is like a wave of the sea, blown and tossed by the wind. That man should not think he will receive anything from the Lord; he is a double-minded man, unstable in all he does'*
(James 1:5-8).

One day two women came before King Solomon. These two women had several things in common: they were both prostitutes, they lived in the same house and they both had recently given birth to a son. During the night prior to their appearance before Solomon, one of the women had accidentally smothered her son while sleeping. The woman who woke up to find the dead baby in her bed accused the other woman of taking her healthy son during the night and replacing him with the dead child. Of course, the other woman denied these charges. These two women found themselves in the midst of a vicious dispute which they could not resolve on their own, and so they came to King Solomon hoping that he could settle the matter. When they appeared before him, both women continued to claim to be the mother of the living son. How would Solomon resolve this matter? How could he determine the identity of the true mother? How could he tell which of the women was lying?

After hearing their case, King Solomon responded by barking out an order to his servants: 'Bring me a sword' (1 Kings 3:24). When the sword was brought, he commanded his servants to cut the living child in two and split the two halves between the women. After hearing this shocking command, one of the women immediately exclaimed, 'Please, my lord, give her the living baby! Don't kill him!' (v. 26). The other woman, however, responded by crying out, 'Neither I nor you shall have him. Cut him in two!' (v. 26). After hearing these two responses, King Solomon pronounced his judgement: 'Give the living baby to the first woman. Do not kill him; she is his mother' (v. 27). When the news of Solomon's actions spread throughout Israel the people held the king in awe, 'because they saw that he had wisdom from God to administer justice' (v. 28).

Obviously, most of us have never had to face a dilemma like the one faced by Solomon, but all of us have faced, and will face, many challenging and perplexing decisions in the course of our lives. Life is full of dilemmas and challenging choices. Where should I go to college? What career should I choose? Whom should I marry? Which job should I take? How should I educate my children? Should I have this surgery? How will I endure this trial? In order to answer such questions and successfully navigate the troubled waters of this life, we need what Solomon possessed — wisdom from God.

As we have seen, in the opening verses of his epistle Pastor James calls his congregation to an incredibly high standard — perfection. His pastoral desire is to see his flock become 'mature and complete, not lacking anything' (James 1:4). However, James knew that his flock was lacking something which was preventing them from attaining this level of Christian maturity. He focuses in on what his congregation was lacking by repeating the Greek verb 'to lack' (*leipo*) in the verse which immediately follows his call for them to be 'mature and complete, not *lacking* anything' (James 1:4, emphasis mine). The next verse begins with the phrase 'If any of you *lacks* [*leipo*] wisdom' (v. 5, emphasis mine). This was James' subtle method of revealing to his congregation what they needed most; he told them that what they lacked was wisdom.

James' message regarding the need for wisdom is just as relevant for us today as it was to its original hearers. Like James' congregation, modern Christians are also in desperate need of wisdom. Thankfully, James reveals to us how to meet this need. In his epistle, he answers four important questions regarding wisdom: what it is, how we can acquire it, why we lack it, and why we need wisdom. In this chapter, we'll look at James' answer to the first two of these questions. We will answer the final two questions in the following chapter.

## What is wisdom?

While most of us desire to be wise, few of us could define what wisdom is. Wisdom is a difficult concept to define. We would have an even harder time defining what James meant by wisdom, because James lived in a very different world from the one in which we live. In order to understand his definition we must step back into his world. But how can we, who are nearly two millennia removed from the writing of the epistle of James, step back in time and find out what he meant? We can do it by examining how wisdom was understood in James' Bible (his version of the Old Testament) and by examining how the concept of wisdom functions elsewhere in his epistle.

## Wisdom in James' Bible

James' primary Bible was the Greek version of the Old Testament known as the 'Septuagint'. The fact that James used this version of the Old Testament is very helpful to our inquiry, because his epistle was also written in Greek. Therefore, we can take the Greek word for 'wisdom' used in James 1:5 and search for its use in the Septuagint. This search should give us clues regarding how James understood the concept.

The Greek word translated as 'wisdom' in James 1:5 is the word *sophia. Sophia* is employed frequently in the Septuagint.[1] One of the places where it appears with some frequency is in the section of the book of Exodus which deals with the construction of the tabernacle.[2] In this section, *sophia* is employed particularly with reference to the craftsmen who carried out the construction. I think it is this specific use of *sophia* which sheds the most light on what James meant by wisdom.

Let us take a closer look at how wisdom was used in this section of Exodus. Consider, for example, the use of *sophia* in Exodus 36:1:

> So Bezalel, Oholiab and every skilled person to whom the LORD has given skill [*sophia*] and ability to know how to carry out all the work of constructing the sanctuary are to do the work just as the LORD has commanded.

The first thing to note about the use of *sophia* in this text is how it is translated. Instead of being translated as 'wisdom', *sophia* is translated as 'skill'. This tells us that, in the Bible that James used, wisdom was related to the concept of skill. In particular, *sophia* referred to the skill necessary to carry out a task according to God's command. Note that Bezalel and Oholiab were given *sophia* ('skill') in order to '*know how to carry out* all the work of constructing the sanctuary' (Exodus 36:1, emphasis mine).

In other words, according to Exodus, wisdom is the ability to skilfully apply God's will to real-life situations — like building the tabernacle. God commanded Bezalel and Oholiab to build his sanctuary, and he equipped them with wisdom to complete this task. Their job was to put God's Word to work in the real world. This is how James understands the concept of wisdom. It is putting God's Word to work in our everyday lives.

## Wisdom in the epistle of James

According to James, wisdom involves action — it is not simply about knowing; it is also about doing. That James understood wisdom in this manner is supported by his discussion of wisdom in another section of his epistle. As previously noted, James follows a pattern of introducing a main topic in the first chapter of his epistle and then returning to it later on in the epistle. James follows this pattern with the topic of wisdom. He first introduces the topic in James 1:5-8 and then revisits it in James 3:13-18. Note what James says about wisdom in this latter text:

> Who is wise and understanding among you? Let him show it by his good life, by deeds done in the humility that comes from wisdom. But if you harbour bitter envy and selfish ambition in your hearts, do not boast about it or deny the truth. Such 'wisdom' does not come down from heaven but is earthly, unspiritual, of the devil. For where you have envy and selfish ambition, there you find disorder and every evil practice.
>
> But the wisdom that comes from heaven is first of all pure; then peace-loving, considerate, submissive, full of mercy and good fruit, impartial and sincere. Peacemakers who sow in peace raise a harvest of righteousness.

This section, in which James contrasts heavenly and earthly wisdom, displays the connection between wisdom and action in two ways.

First, James makes an explicit connection between wisdom and action in the opening verse of this section: 'Who is wise and understanding among you? *Let him show it by his good life, by deeds done in the humility that comes from wisdom*' (James 3:13, emphasis mine). According to James, wisdom manifests itself in the active living of the 'good life' and in 'deeds done in humility'. These are the actions which come 'from wisdom'.

Second, James displays the connection between wisdom and action by means of his contrast between heavenly and earthly wisdom. According to James, these two forms of wisdom both yield various actions. For example, heavenly wisdom manifests itself in godly actions such as a good life (v. 13), humility (v. 13), purity (v. 17), peace (v. 17), consideration of others (v. 17), submissiveness (v. 17), mercy (v. 17), good fruit (v. 17), impartiality (v. 17) and sincerity (v. 17). In contrast, earthly wisdom produces evil actions such as bitter envy (v. 14), selfish ambition (v. 14), disorder (v. 16) and every evil practice (v. 16).

As we can see from the use of wisdom in the Old Testament and from its use in James 3:13-18, James understood wisdom in practical terms. For James, wisdom is about doing. It is about taking God's Word and applying it to all the aspects of the Christian life. Our world is to be shaped by his Word. This understanding of wisdom is entirely consistent with the thrust of the entire epistle of James which emphasizes so forcefully the *doing* of God's Word. Wisdom, according to James, is the ability to skilfully apply the Word of God to real-world situations.

## How do we acquire wisdom?

Knowing what James meant by wisdom should lead us to yearn to possess it. After all, what Christian would not desire the ability to skilfully apply the Word of God to real-life situations? Therefore, the next question which logically arises is: 'How do we acquire wisdom?' Pastor James anticipated that his congregation would ask this very same question, and so he provided them with the answer in James 1:5: 'If any of you lacks wisdom, *he should ask God*, who gives generously to all without finding fault, and it will be given to him' (emphasis mine). James tells us that we acquire wisdom by asking God for it.

It is important to note that when James calls us to ask God for wisdom he is not saying that all we have to do is ask once. The Greek word which is translated as 'ask' in James 1:5 is a present imperative verb. This means that our asking must be a continual aspect of the Christian life. We must ask God repeatedly for wisdom as we encounter each new challenge and dilemma. Jesus emphasizes a similar point in Luke 11:9-10 where he instructs his disciples how to pray:

'So I say to you: Ask and it will be given to you; seek and you will find; knock and the door will be opened to you. For everyone who asks receives; he who seeks finds; and to him who knocks, the door will be opened.'

As in James 1:5, the verbs used by Jesus for asking ('ask', 'seek' and 'knock') are all present imperative verbs. Jesus, like James, calls us to continually seek God for our needs. If we want wisdom, all we have to do is ask.

## The example of Solomon

I began this chapter with an illustration from the life of Solomon. I did this because Solomon is world-renowned for his wisdom. Foreign dignitaries, such as the Queen of Sheba, travelled great distances to benefit from his advice. Solomon also wrote books of wisdom. Many scholars believe that he authored all or parts of the major wisdom books of the Old Testament, such as Proverbs, Song of Solomon and Ecclesiastes. Even in our modern post-Christian world, the name 'Solomon' is still nearly synonymous with wisdom. The English dictionary even includes the word 'Solomonic', which denotes a person who acts wisely. Clearly, Solomon was an extraordinarily wise man. But have you ever wondered how he became so wise? The Bible reveals his secret. The Bible tells us that Solomon acquired his wisdom in the exact manner set forth by James — Solomon asked God for it.

In fact, the Bible records the exact moment when Solomon asked God for wisdom. Solomon's request for wisdom is found in 1 Kings 3:5-9 (emphasis mine):

> At Gibeon the LORD appeared to Solomon during the night in a dream, and God said, 'Ask for whatever you want me to give you.'
>
> Solomon answered, 'You have shown great kindness to your servant, my father David, because he was faithful to you and righteous and upright in heart. You have continued this great kindness to him and have given him a son to sit on his throne this very day.
>
> 'Now, O LORD my God, you have made your servant king in place of my father David. But I am only a little child and do not know how to carry out my duties. Your servant is here among the people you have chosen, a great people, too numerous to count or number. *So give your servant a discerning heart to govern your people and to distinguish between right and wrong.* For who is able to govern this great people of yours?'

In this text, we learn that God appeared to Solomon in a dream and said, 'Ask for whatever you want me to give you' (v. 5). Pause and think about God's offer for a moment. What an incredible opportunity for Solomon! God offered Solomon one request and Solomon could have asked for 'whatever' he wanted. He could have asked God for wealth, long life or fame. Yet he did not ask for such things; instead he asked for wisdom. Solomon recognized that he could not carry out his duties as a king by relying on his own wisdom and so he asked God to give him a 'discerning heart' and the ability to 'distinguish between right and wrong' (v. 9). Solomon received wisdom because he asked God for it.

## The generous giver

Now I realize that some of you may be thinking at this point, 'It just seems too simple. How can such a precious gift like wisdom be so easy to acquire?' James answers this question by shifting our focus away from the one who *asks* for wisdom to the one who *gives* wisdom. Note this shift in James 1:5: 'If any of you lacks wisdom, he should ask God, *who gives generously to all without finding fault, and it will be given to him*' (emphasis mine). Wisdom is so easy to acquire because the giver of wisdom is incredibly generous. James tells us that God is universally generous to his children — he 'gives generously to all'. In fact, God is so generous in giving wisdom that he is even willing to overlook our sinfulness. James tells us that God gives wisdom 'without finding fault'.

James Adamson writes:

> God gives his wisdom to men not only just for the asking but also without chiding man for his previous sins.[3]

What a wonderful God we serve! What a generous and gracious Father! When we ask him for wisdom he stands ready and willing to give it to us in bounteous proportions. Once again we see this principle illustrated in the life of Solomon.

After Solomon asked God for the gift of wisdom, the Bible records the fact that God was 'pleased that Solomon had asked for this' (1 Kings 3:10). God warmly welcomed Solomon's prayer, and he rejoiced in answering it. Note God's display of generosity in his answer to Solomon's prayer in the verses which follow:

So God said to him, 'Since you have asked for this and not for long life or wealth for yourself, nor have asked for the death of your enemies but for discernment in administering justice, I will do what you have asked. I will give you a wise and discerning heart, so that there will never have been anyone like you, nor will there ever be. Moreover, I will give you what you have not asked for — both riches and honour — so that in your lifetime you will have no equal among kings. And if you walk in my ways and obey my statutes and commands as David your father did, I will give you a long life'

(1 Kings 3:11-14).

As you can see from God's response, he not only gave Solomon a 'wise and discerning heart', but he was so pleased that Solomon prized wisdom above all things that he also granted him many other blessings as well. Our God is a generous God. He is pleased by our prayers for wisdom and stands ready and willing to answer them.

By focusing on the generosity of God in answering our prayers, James is once again repeating instruction which he received directly from Jesus. In Luke 11, after teaching his disciples how to pray, Jesus reminds them about the generous nature of their heavenly Father in answering their prayers:

'Which of you fathers, if your son asks for a fish, will give him a snake instead? Or if he asks for an egg, will give him a scorpion? If you then, though you are evil, know how to give good gifts to your children, *how much more will your Father in heaven give the Holy Spirit to those who ask him!'*

(Luke 11:11-13, emphasis mine).

Jesus, like James, reminds us that our God is a generous Father who gives good gifts to his children. How do we acquire wisdom? According to James, all we have to do is ask and 'it will be given' to us.

# 6.
# Wisdom and the Christian life
# – Part 2

*'If any of you lacks wisdom, he should ask God, who gives generously to all without finding fault, and it will be given to him. But when he asks, he must believe and not doubt, because he who doubts is like a wave of the sea, blown and tossed by the wind. That man should not think he will receive anything from the Lord; he is a double-minded man, unstable in all he does'*
(James 1:5-8).

In the previous chapter we examined the first two of the four questions James addresses regarding wisdom and the Christian life. First we looked at what wisdom is, and we learned that James defines wisdom as the ability to skilfully apply the Word of God to real-life situations. Wisdom involves applying God's Word to our world. Next we looked at how we acquire wisdom, and we learned that wisdom is acquired by simply asking our generous heavenly Father for it. In this chapter, we'll explore James' answer to the final two questions he addresses regarding wisdom and the Christian life — first, why we lack wisdom; and second, why we need it.

## Why do we lack wisdom?

James has taught us that acquiring wisdom is incredibly easy. God does not require us to jump through a series of hoops, but rather he simply gives it to us when we ask. But if wisdom is so easy to acquire, then why does it seem like the church is in desperate need of it? As a pastor, I have observed that Christians frequently seem unable to navigate life's troubled waters using the compass of God's Word. The modern church is being crippled by the widespread inability of Christians to successfully apply God's Word to the real world. Something is lacking, and that something is the gift of wisdom. Much like the congregation to which James wrote, we too are lacking wisdom. But the question is '*Why?*' Why are Christians lacking wisdom when all they have to do to acquire it is to ask God for it?

Pastor James anticipated that his congregation would be asking the same question, and so he addresses this question in James 1:6-8: 'But when he asks, he must believe and not doubt, because he who doubts is like a wave of the sea, blown and tossed by the wind. That man should not think he will receive anything from the Lord; he is a double-minded man, unstable in all he does.' According to James, the reason we lack wisdom is because we are 'double-minded' when we ask God for it. What exactly does James mean by the term 'double-minded'? Let me try to shed some light on this concept by means of an illustration from the world of espionage.

## Spiritual double agents

He began working at the CIA in the early 1960s and continued to work for the intelligence agency for thirty-one years. His career was marked by mediocrity and obscurity. He never reached beyond the status of a mid-level employee. However, in 1985 he did something which would eventually make him notorious. In that year, Aldrich Ames made his first sale of United States secrets to the Soviet Union. Over the next nine years Ames became rich by selling out his country. He committed treason against his nation. He was finally exposed as a double agent in 1994. Aldrich Ames became the most infamous double agent in American history.

The concept of a double agent is helpful in understanding what James meant by the phrase 'double-minded'.[1] A double agent is an agent who is working simultaneously for two sovereign governments which are ultimately at odds with one another. A double agent has divided loyalties and no real commitment to anyone except himself. This is very similar to what James has in mind when he introduces the concept of the double-minded man. The double-minded man, like a double agent, is simultaneously working for two governments — the government of God and the government of Satan. A double-minded man has one foot in the world and one foot in the church. A double-minded man is a *spiritual* double agent. Such a man suffers from what one commentator refers to as 'spiritual schizophrenia'.[2] The Puritan John Bunyan referred to the double-minded man as 'Mr. Facing-both-ways'.[3]

Now that we better understand the nature of the 'double-minded' man, the next question which arises is this: Why does spiritual double-mindedness lead to ineffective requests for wisdom? James answers this question through a maritime illustration.


## Like the waves of the sea

I love the water. I enjoy simply watching the waves sway back and forth. In a natural sense, this swaying action of the waves is both soothing and beautiful. However, in a spiritual sense it is a negative action. God does not want our hearts to be like the waves of the sea.

In James 1:6 James likens the prayers of the double-minded man to 'a wave of the sea, blown and tossed by the wind.' Here he informs us that the double-minded man not only lives his life with divided loyalties, but he also prays to God with a divided heart. Like the waves of the sea, the prayers of the double-minded man sway endlessly back and forth between belief and unbelief, faithfulness and unfaithfulness, trustfulness and distrust. James Adamson explains how the vacillating dynamic of the heart of the double-minded man mimics the ever-swaying waves of the sea:

> The doubter here inclines (but no more) toward one alternative (say, to believe in prayer) and then inclines (but no more) toward the opposite alternative, and never is able to settle upon either: he is thus in constant agitation without making any progress to any result.[4]

Dan Doriani explains it this way: 'The doubter asks God for aid, but before he finishes his prayer, he thinks, "This will never work." He vacillates, tossing from one idea to the next, with no more stability of direction or purpose than a wind-whipped wave.'[5] The double-minded man's prayers are filled with endless agitation and instability.

## No one can serve two masters

The reason that the double-minded man lacks wisdom is that he fails to ask God with a committed and believing heart. He fails to make his requests with single-minded sincerity, but rather makes them with double-minded doubt. Remember,

God demands that we love him with *all* our hearts, *all* our souls and *all* our strength (Deuteronomy 6:5). As Jesus taught us, we simply cannot serve two masters: 'No one can serve two masters. Either he will hate the one and love the other, or he will be devoted to the one and despise the other' (Matthew 6:24). James tells us that we often lack wisdom because we are trying to serve two diametrically opposed masters.

For James there is no middle ground when it comes to our loyalties. He makes this abundantly clear in the stern words of James 4:4: 'You adulterous people, don't you know that friendship with the world is hatred towards God? Anyone who chooses to be a friend of the world becomes an enemy of God.' According to James, God will brook no rivals. He will not grant the divine gift of wisdom to those with divided loyalties, to those who are consorting with the enemy.

Ultimately, James views double-mindedness in prayer as an indication of a lack of faith in God. According to James, a prayer offered without the single-minded conviction that God will answer it is a prayer that will go unanswered. Douglas Moo writes, 'Our asking must coincide with the way in which God gives: he gives with singleness of intent; we must ask with singleness of intent.'[6] James is not demanding that our faith be perfect or that we must be free from all doubt in order to receive wisdom; but, rather, what he demands is that we pray with confident, committed and convinced hearts. Here again James is merely echoing the teaching of his brother Jesus who placed a similar condition on our prayers:

Mark 11:24:     'Therefore I tell you, whatever you ask for in prayer, *believe that you have received it*, and it will be yours' (emphasis mine).

Matthew 21:22:   '*If you believe*, you will receive whatever you ask for in prayer' (emphasis mine).

The reason we lack wisdom is because we are double-minded in our lives, loyalties and, most of all, in our prayers.

Do you seem incapable of navigating life's troubled waters? Are you unable to apply the principles of God's Word to the challenges and dilemmas which emerge in your life? Do your prayers for wisdom seem to go unanswered? If so, then perhaps it is time that you engaged in some spiritual self-assessment. Perhaps it is time that you asked yourself questions like the following: Am I serving two masters? Am I keeping one foot in the church and the other in the world? Am I a double-minded Christian? Am I suffering from 'spiritual schizophrenia'? Do my prayers vacillate like the waves of seas? Am I unstable in all my ways?

In the Old Testament, Joshua forced the people of God to make a choice regarding their loyalties. He demanded that they make a decision regarding whom they would serve — God or the world. Joshua left absolutely no doubt that he was a single-minded man when he declared, 'as for me and my household, we will serve the LORD' (Joshua 24:15). Have you made that choice? Whom are you serving? Who owns your time, talent and treasure? Where do your loyalties rest? Remember, James warns us that a double-minded man 'should not think he will receive anything from the Lord' (James 1:7). The reason we lack wisdom, according to James, is because we are so often serving as spiritual double agents.

## Why do we need wisdom?

Thus far in our study of James 1:5-8 we have learned about the nature of wisdom, how to acquire it and why we so often lack it. However, one final question remains regarding the topic of wisdom. Why do we need it? What purpose does wisdom serve in the Christian life? Why does James put such a great emphasis on the need for wisdom in his letter to this suffering community?

There are, of course, many reasons why we need wisdom in the Christian life. Wisdom aids us in choosing between alternatives. It assists us in our stewardship of the money God has given to us. It guides us in choosing a spouse and selecting a vocation. It enlightens us regarding how to raise our children. Wisdom is a multifaceted tool — a kind of Swiss army knife of the mind. J. A. Motyer describes the wise man as a man who 'knows how to *use* his Bible to understand life and the world around him, and to guide his own conduct and the conduct of others in the maze of life's problems'.[7] Wisdom enables us to deal successfully with a vast array of problems. We need wisdom to live the Christian life. The reasons why we need wisdom are simply too many to number.

However, while wisdom has many functions in the Christian life, James has one very specific function in mind in James 1:5-8. As you will recall, James began the main body of his epistle with these words: 'Consider it pure joy, my brothers, *whenever you face trials* of many kinds' (1:2, emphasis mine). James first raises the topic of wisdom in a section of his epistle dealing with trials. By beginning his discussion of wisdom here, James is telling us that wisdom is absolutely vital for guiding us through our trials.

So exactly how does wisdom help us through those trials? It helps us by allowing us to see the big picture. It helps us to understand God's blueprint for our lives. Let me illustrate what I mean.

## Seeing the big picture

When the Hoyts' son, Rick, was born, the doctors told them that he would be a 'vegetable' for life.[8] Rick had suffered brain damage as a result of being strangled by the umbilical cord during his birth. Because of this brain damage, Rick was unable to control his limbs and to communicate verbally. When he was nine months old his doctors recommended that his parents put him in an institution. For the Hoyts, the joy of having a son was quickly transformed into a challenging trial. I would imagine that they struggled with the meaning and purpose of this trial, not least with the questions, 'Why has this happened to our son? Why has this happened to us?'

The Hoyts, however, refused to accept the diagnosis and recommendations of their doctors. They began to notice that Rick's eyes would follow them around the room and that he would laugh at their jokes. Eventually, they were able to configure a system whereby Rick could communicate with them through a computer. One day, Rick expressed a desire to participate in a marathon. His father, Dick, agreed to this and commenced training for the event. Soon Dick and his son were entering numerous marathons, and they later moved on to compete in triathlons. By 2005, they had participated in a staggering total of 212 triathlons. During every one of these competitions, Dick would carry, tow and haul his son through these gruelling events.[9]

The fact that Dick and Rick were able to complete 212 triathlons is an incredible feat in its own right. However, there is more to this story. In 2003, Dick suffered a mild heart attack during a triathlon. The doctors informed him that one of his arteries was almost completely blocked and that he would have died years ago if he had not been in such great physical condition. It was Rick's disability which inspired Dick to get into such great physical shape, and this conditioning ultimately saved his life.

## Seeing the top of the canvas

When we experience a trial like that experienced by the Hoyts, we often struggle to make sense of God's plan for our lives.

Sometimes, as in the case of the Hoyts, we can eventually see the wisdom of our trials in this lifetime. We can see how God worked all things together for good (Romans 8:28). Other times, however, we are not able to fully make sense of God's plan in this life. Sometimes God's actions simply don't compute in our finite minds. In his commentary on James, Kent Hughes includes an insightful poem from an unknown author, which illustrates this dynamic. The poem compares God's work in constructing the plan of our lives to that of a weaver creating a canvas and, from our perspective, we can only see the underside of the canvas:

> My life is but a weaving,
> Between my Lord and me;
> I cannot choose the colours.
> He worketh steadily.
>
> Oftentimes He weaveth sorrow
> And I in foolish pride,
> Forget he sees the upper
> And I the under side.
>
> Not till the loom is silent
> And the shuttle cease to fly,
> Shall God unroll the canvas
> And explain the reason why.
>
> The dark threads are as needful
> In the Weaver's skilful hand,
> As the threads of gold and silver,
> In the pattern He has planned.[10]

It is when we cannot see the upper side of the canvas that wisdom becomes so valuable. Divine wisdom allows us to trust that our present trials, no matter how incomprehensible they seem, are part of the eternal purposes of a good and gracious God. As Peter Davids puts it: 'Wisdom ... is the possession of the believer given by the Spirit that enables him to see history from the divine perspective.'[11] It is wisdom from God which enables us to respond to our trials with pure joy (James 1:2-4) and patience (James 5:7-11). Wisdom allows us to see the top side of the canvas.

## Becoming a skilled craftsman

Think back for a moment to Bezalel and Oholiab, those two skilled craftsmen who built the tabernacle (Exodus 36:1). The blueprint for the tabernacle came directly from the mind of God. Bezalel and Oholiab were not the architects; rather, they were called to apply God's knowledge to the real-life task of building it. God equipped and gifted them with wisdom in order to carry out this task. Through God's gift of wisdom, Bezalel and Oholiab were able to make sense of God's plan for the tabernacle. They came to understand how its various parts fit together. They were enabled to comprehend the big picture.

A similar dynamic occurs in the Christian life. God gives us wisdom to enable us to make sense of his plan for our lives. Wisdom enables us to see the big picture, and this allows us to persevere and to trust God even in the midst of trials of many kinds.

Why do we need wisdom? We need wisdom to help us make sense of our trials in the gritty realities of our daily lives. We need wisdom to thrive in the trenches of our trials. We need wisdom so that we too can become like Bezalel and Oholiab, who not only understood the big picture, but who also became skilled craftsmen in applying God's Word to the real world in which they lived.

## The one greater than Solomon

As Pastor James wrote to his suffering congregation and called them to consider their trials as 'pure joy', he knew that he was calling them to an incredibly difficult task. James knew that his flock needed more than theological principles to make sense of their trials — he knew that they needed wisdom from God.

My guess is that some of you who are reading this book are struggling with trials. Maybe you are on the brink of making a major life-altering decision, or perhaps you feel trapped by a perplexing problem that seems to have no apparent solution. At times like these James counsels us to ask God for wisdom. He instructs us to go to our generous heavenly Father, with a devoted and loyal heart, and ask him for the precious gift of wisdom.

In the previous chapter I used the illustration of Solomon, who is world renowned for possessing the gift of wisdom. But the New Testament tells us that Jesus is even greater and wiser than King Solomon (Luke 11:31). James is telling you that in the midst of your trials you must go to King Jesus and ask him for the gift of wisdom. He is a very wise King, and he loves you. He will not only provide you with mercy and grace in your time of need, but he will also provide you with wisdom. Just go to him and ask.

# 7.

# Reversal of fortunes:

# a proper perspective on prosperity

*'The brother in humble circumstances ought to take pride in his high position. But the one who is rich should take pride in his low position, because he will pass away like a wild flower. For the sun rises with scorching heat and withers the plant; its blossom falls and its beauty is destroyed. In the same way, the rich man will fade away even while he goes about his business,'*
(James 1:9-11).

G. K. Chesterton's classic book, *Orthodoxy*, includes a chapter entitled 'The Paradoxes of Christianity'. In this chapter of his book, Chesterton explains that one of Christianity's strengths is that it is an inherently logical and reasonable faith. However, he goes on to suggest that Christianity's *greatest* strength is not the fact that it reveals logical truth, but rather that it reveals 'illogical truth'.[1] According to Chesterton, Christianity is most profound when it enables us to comprehend truths which completely contradict the principles of this world. Chesterton suggests that one of the ways that Christianity conveys 'illogical truth' is through its many paradoxes.

What is a paradox? A paradox is a statement that seems contradictory. At first glance, a paradox simply does not compute to our minds and defies all that we think we know about how the world works. Chesterton provides an example of a paradox in his chapter on this subject.

He invites us to imagine that a fictional 'mathematical creature' ventures from the moon and comes to visit earth. When the creature arrives on earth he begins to study the nature of mankind. The creature begins to see a pattern in the anatomy of man. He notes that man has two arms, two legs, two sets of fingers, two sets of toes, two eyes, two ears, two nostrils and even two lobes of the brain. Based on this observable data the creature arrives at the seemingly reasonable conclusion that man is really a duplicate possessing two sides that are exactly the same. The creature then formulates the following universal law: 'A man is two men, he on the right exactly resembling him on the left.'[2] This seems like an inherently logical conclusion.

However, just when the creature thinks he has fully comprehended the essence of the nature of mankind, he takes a glance at the heart of man and, much to his surprise, he finds one heart on the left side of the man, but no corresponding heart on his right side. At this moment the creature's universal law collapses like a house of cards. He encountered something that did not compute with his reasoning. Chesterton describes the creature's shock: 'And just then, where he most felt he was right, he would be wrong.'[3]

Like Chesterton's mathematical creature, we often think we have everything figured out. We too assume that we understand the laws of the universe. The congregation to whom James wrote also thought they had everything figured out, particularly with regard to what makes one great in this world. They assumed, much like we continue to assume today, that what makes one great in this world is the amount of money one possesses. James informs his congregation that those who are rich are, in fact, truly poor, and those who are poor are, in fact, truly rich. He reveals to them a great reversal of fortune. He unfolds for them the wealth of the impoverished and the poverty of the wealthy. He reveals 'illogical truth' to them by means of two paradoxical propositions.

## The wealth of the impoverished

The first paradox set forth by James is that the poor of this world are, in reality, the truly wealthy. He reveals this principle in James 1:9 where he declares that, 'The brother in humble circumstances ought to take pride in his high position.' In this context, the Greek word translated as 'humble' refers specifically to the socio-economic status of the brother, rather than to a general attitude of humility. In other words, the brother in 'humble circumstances' is economically poor. Yet James declares that this brother, who is low in the eyes of the world, is actually residing in a 'high position.' In fact, James indicates that this lowly impoverished brother is in such an exalted status that he ought to take pride in it! This call to be proud in poverty becomes even more shocking when we recall that pride is so frequently condemned in the New Testament.[4] James tells his congregation that the impoverished believer is the richest of all people and that he should boast in his exalted state. According to James, it is the poor who are truly wealthy. This is indeed a paradoxical principle.

Once again, James is simply echoing the teaching of his brother. This section of the epistle of James reads much like Jesus' words in the Beatitudes. Consider, for example, Matthew 5:3-5: 'Blessed are the poor in spirit, for theirs is the kingdom of heaven. Blessed are those who mourn, for they will be comforted. Blessed are the meek, for they will inherit the earth.' This paradox of the exalted position of the lowly is one of the core themes of the gospel. It is mentioned numerous times, particularly in the Gospel of Luke. For example, in Luke 13:30, Jesus declares, 'Indeed there are those who are last who will be first, and first who will be last.' We also see this paradox affirmed in Mary's Song in which she declares of God, 'He has brought down rulers from their thrones but has lifted up the humble,' (Luke 1:52). Like Jesus, James tells us that it is the poor who will ultimately be enriched and exalted.

## Eternal economics

Now at first glance it would be very easy to take a cynical approach to this paradox offered by James. One could dismiss it as James simply offering his congregation some type of pie-in-the-sky promise to help them get through the hopeless realities of this life. Perhaps James is using religion in a Marxian sense. Perhaps he is offering this paradox as an opiate of the masses in order to keep the poor working class satiated while they are being fleeced by the owners of the means of production. After all, when one looks at our present world, doesn't it seem absolutely absurd to suggest that the poor are truly rich? How can this be true?

When James tells us that it is the poor who are truly rich he is giving us an example of Chesterton's 'illogical truth'. He is trying to show us a reality that we cannot see through the spectacles of this world. James is not offering his people a hollow promise which is intended to get them through this life; rather, his goal is to encourage his flock to look beyond this age and see things as they really are. He is trying to persuade believers to interpret their present circumstances as if they were already residing in glory. Peter Davids notes that James is calling the Christian to 'overlook the present circumstances in which it is the rich who boast ... and see life from an eschatological perspective in which the one who really has the exalted position and who is really rich is the Christian...'[5] James is demanding that we view wealth and poverty in the light of eternal realities. He is calling us to apply eternal economics to this present age.

When we apply eternal economics to this present age we quickly come to recognize how truly rich we are. By looking to the age to come we realize that we are in present possession of a fully vested interest in the greatest inheritance of all — the glorious riches of Jesus Christ! The apostle Peter declares to us in 1 Peter 1:4 that all Christians presently possess 'an inheritance that can never perish, spoil or fade' which is 'kept in heaven' for us. It is because we have this present interest in the inheritance of Christ that James can say sincerely that, 'The brother in humble circumstances ought to take pride in his high position,' (1:9).

Every year *Fortune* magazine compiles a list of the world's wealthiest people. These individuals are ranked by the amount of earthly wealth they possess. James reminds us that this is the wrong metric for measuring wealth. He asserts that the most impoverished Christian is wealthier than any unbeliever on such a list because it is only the Christian who has the right to declare himself a co-heir with Jesus Christ (Romans 8:17). So, in this first paradoxical statement, James reminds us of the illogical truth that the poor in Christ are the truly rich.

## The poverty of the wealthy

In James 1:10-11, James unfolds the second part of his paradox by revealing to us the poverty of the wealthy. In verse 10 he declares, 'But the one who is rich should take pride in his low position.' He informs the rich that they have nothing. According to James, the wealthy are actually in a low position. He tells them that they are truly poor.

Once again, at first glance this statement seems utterly nonsensical. How can the rich be deemed to have nothing? James answers this question by once again forcing us to view wealth in the light of eternal realities. When we look at earthly wealth with heavenly eyes we quickly realize how insignificant and fleeting it is. We recognize that wealth is an entirely temporal phenomenon. James demonstrates this reality to us by means of an agricultural illustration.

## Wealth is like a wild flower

At the end of verse 10, James compares a rich man to a flower. He declares that the rich man will 'pass away like a wild flower'. He then proceeds to explain how this will happen: 'For the sun rises with scorching heat and withers the plant; its blossom falls and its beauty is destroyed' (v. 11). Do you see James' point here? He is showing that earthly wealth is fleeting. Earthly wealth is like the glory of the wild flower; it exists for only a brief time and then it is gone.[6] The scorching heat rapidly destroys its beauty. James concludes that a similar thing happens to the rich man: 'In the same way, the rich man will fade away even while he goes about his business' (1:11). Just like the wild flower the rich man may appear arrayed in beauty in this life, but in the vastness of eternity his beauty drops off like a blossom in the scorching heat. When earthly wealth is appraised from an eternal perspective it is deemed worthless. This is why the rich man is, in reality, eternally impoverished.

## You can't take it with you

At one level, the paradoxical principle James is teaching here is a matter of universal wisdom. It appears in other parts of the Bible.

For example, consider these words from Psalm 49:16: 'Do not be overawed when a man grows rich, when the splendour of his house increases; for he will take nothing with him when he dies, his splendour will not descend with him.' Even our own godless culture understands this truth. Its substance is expressed in the popular cultural proverb, 'You can't take it with you.'

In his commentary on Psalm 49, James Montgomery Boice recounts the following story which illustrates the main point of Psalm 49 and James 1:10-11:

> Two men met in a streetcar one day and began to talk about a millionaire whose death had been announced in the morning's paper. 'How much did he leave?' one asked the other. 'Everything he had!' replied his companion.[7]

The point that Boice was illustrating is that we cannot take our wealth with us into eternity. He goes on to note the old saying that burial 'shrouds have no pockets.'[8]

Even though most of us grasp that we cannot take our wealth with us, we still often subconsciously live our lives as if we can. Even though we know it is impossible to take our possessions with us this does not prevent us from trying. It is so easy to place our trust in our wealth and bestow upon it a significance that it neither deserves nor possesses. James reminds us that placing our trust in our wealth is not only foolish, but it is also eternally dangerous. It threatens our ability to properly live the Christian life. Trusting in wealth can lead us into the perils of prosperity.

## The perils of prosperity

'The perils of prosperity' is one of the main themes of the epistle of James. James is very concerned about this issue because he knows that when Christians place their trust in their wealth they place themselves in peril. When we trust in our wealth rather than in God we violate the two great commandments to love God and to love our neighbour. When we place our trust in our wealth money becomes our god and we often abuse our neighbour to keep and acquire more of it.

In fact, James is so concerned about this danger that he reserves some of the harshest words of his epistle for those who are placing their trust in their wealth. For example, in James 5:1-6, he issues an impassioned prophetic oracle of judgement upon the unrighteous wealthy landowners of his day:

> Now listen, you rich people, weep and wail because of the misery that is coming upon you. Your wealth has rotted, and moths have eaten your clothes. Your gold and silver are corroded. Their corrosion will testify against you and eat your flesh like fire. You have hoarded wealth in the last days. Look! The wages you failed to pay the workmen who mowed your fields are crying out against you. The cries of the harvesters have reached the ears of the Lord Almighty. You have lived on earth in luxury and self-indulgence. You have fattened yourselves in the day of slaughter. You have condemned and murdered innocent men, who were not opposing you.

Here James powerfully echoes the prophets of the Old Testament by issuing this oracle of judgement against those who are taking pride in their wealth and using it as a tool to oppress others. Just as he did in James 1:10-11, James reminds the rich that their wealth is temporary: 'Your wealth has rotted, and moths have eaten your clothes. Your gold and silver are corroded' (James 5:2-3).[9]

James declares to the rich that they are in fact impoverished. He tells them that they possess nothing of lasting value. He also warns them that the return of Jesus Christ will make their true spiritual poverty readily apparent, 'Now listen, you rich people, weep and wail because of the misery that is coming upon you' (James 5:1). James reminds all those who boast in their riches that the scorching heat of the Son's coming will make them wither like a wild flower.

## So is it sinful to be rich?

After encountering this section of James' epistle it would be easy to conclude that wealth is inherently evil. Clearly, James has some very harsh things to say about wealthy people. In fact, if the Bible's only comment on riches was found here in the epistle of James one might conclude that it is expressly sinful for a Christian to be wealthy. However, such a conclusion would be in error. The Bible does not condemn wealth *per se* nor does it prohibit Christians from acquiring it. In fact, when we reflect on the entirety of Scripture, we find numerous places where the accumulation of wealth is an indication of God's favour and blessing. God often enriches his people. Think of how God enriched Abraham (Genesis 13:2) and how he provided the Israelites with the spoils of Egypt. Both David and Solomon were given great wealth. The book of Proverbs reminds us that a 'good man' is one who leaves an inheritance to his children (Proverbs 13:22). It was the wealthy man Boaz who was able to redeem Ruth and her mother-in-law Naomi. Wealthy people like Phoebe, Lydia, and Aquila and Priscilla were used by God to support and advance the missionary efforts of the gospel. Clearly, the Bible does not teach that wealth is inherently evil.

If the Bible does not condemn wealth then why does James seem to have nothing good to say about wealth or the wealthy? It is because in his epistle James was dealing pastorally with a specific problem regarding the abuse of wealth which had arisen in the context of the congregation to which he was writing.

Accordingly, when James addresses the topic of wealth his goal is not to provide us with a balanced view of the entire biblical perspective on wealth, but rather to warn us about the perils of its misuse. James' pastoral purpose was to correct a group of rich people who were trusting solely in their wealth and using it as a tool to oppress others.

## James' warning and us

Although James was specifically addressing a narrow issue in his congregation regarding the topic of wealth, this does not mean that his warnings about the dangers of trusting in wealth have no application to us today. In fact, James' warnings about the perils of prosperity are quite relevant to our modern age, particularly for those living in the affluent West. When James was writing, wealth was primarily concentrated in the few who were 'upper class'. The overwhelming majority of people were poor. In our day, however, with the rise of the middle class and modern capitalism, the vast majority of people living in the developed world fit quite comfortably into James' category of the 'rich'. In other words, James' warning is for us. It is a warning applicable to all those who are tempted to trust in material wealth and grant it an eternal significance which it does not merit. That describes all of us.

Just think about it for a few moments. How many Christians join in the cultural admiration and adulation bestowed upon the wealthy in our society? How many of us revere athletes and entertainers simply because they are wealthy? How many Christians are attracted to wealthy mega-churches simply because they offer a variety of modern conveniences and consumer choices? How many Christians trust in their bank and investment accounts? How many Christians possess more wealth than their parents, but give a smaller percentage of it to the church? How many of us find our satisfaction in what we possess? Again, the problem is not that we possess wealth, but rather that our wealth often seems to possess us.

Let us not deceive ourselves. Modern Christians are not immune from the perils of prosperity. The alluring power of wealth should never be underestimated. It has a powerful ability to turn our eyes to the things of this world and lead us to treat them as if they are of enduring value. How we view, and what we do with, our wealth and possessions speaks volumes about our spiritual maturity. Therefore, James speaks relevant words to us when he warns us about wealth.

## Avoiding the perils of prosperity

So how do we avoid the perils of prosperity? We avoid them by viewing material wealth with the perspective of eternity and through the eyes of God. This type of supernatural perspective can only be achieved through the gift of heavenly wisdom of which James spoke in James 1:5-8. Only heavenly wisdom can help us to see such 'illogical truth'. Only heavenly wisdom can help us to see things as they really are. J. A. Motyer writes that it is divine wisdom that provides us with the ability 'to see things as they really are, to arrive at true definitions, to cease to live by what appears to be true and to live instead, by what actually is the truth of the matter'.[10]

Wisdom enables us to view the world through eternal spectacles. It empowers us to understand in the here and now the eternal insignificance of earthly treasure. Heavenly wisdom equips us to reject the wisdom of the world which so incessantly begs us to buy into the idea that this world and its wealth are all there is. It is only through the power of wisdom that we are able to grasp the full meaning of the 'illogical truth' of the impoverishment of the wealthy.

## Paradoxes with a purpose

Through the power of paradox, James reminds us to resist viewing this world like Chesterton's mathematical creature viewed the nature of man. James calls us to see the unseen and to anticipate the unexpected. James wants us to develop mature spiritual insight that is not fooled by the illusions of this present age.

G. K. Chesterton noted that true insight is 'best tested by whether it guesses ... hidden malformations and surprises'.[11] He gives an example of what he means by this by returning to his illustration of the mathematical creature. He suggests that if the mathematical creature, after noting that man has two arms, two legs, two sets of fingers, two sets of toes, two eyes, two ears, two nostrils and even two lobes of the brain was then able to guess the proper location of man's heart, and its singularity, then we 'should call him something more than a mathematician'.[12] James was something more than a mathematician and he is calling us to be more than mere mathematicians. James is calling us to display real spiritual insight by being able to see beyond the laws of this world regarding wealth and poverty. Through his paradoxes James invites us to see such 'malformations and surprises' as the reality that the poor in Christ are truly rich and the rich of the world are truly poor.

# 8.
# Triumphing in the tests
# of our temptations

*'Blessed is the man who perseveres under trial, because when he has stood the test, he will receive the crown of life that God has promised to those who love him. When tempted, no one should say, "God is tempting me." For God cannot be tempted by evil, nor does he tempt anyone; but each one is tempted when, by his own evil desire, he is dragged away and enticed. Then, after desire has conceived, it gives birth to sin; and sin, when it is full grown, gives birth to death. Don't be deceived, my dear brothers. Every good and perfect gift is from above, coming down from the Father of the heavenly lights, who does not change like shifting shadows. He chose to give us birth through the word of truth, that we might be a kind of firstfruits of all he created'*
(James 1:12-18).

I recall vividly the gruelling agony of my two-day-long attorney licensing exam known as the 'bar exam'. I took this test in a poorly air-conditioned college classroom in the middle of a hot July. By the end of the exam my hands were cramped from the vigorous and voluminous writing. I remember the tremendous relief I felt after I had completed it. The test was over. However, it wasn't really over because I had to wait until the middle of December, five months later, to find out whether I had passed. For five months I hung in limbo, unsure of whether I had passed or failed.

In James 1:12-18, Pastor James returns to the theme of trials, a theme which he began to explore in James 1:2-4. In verse 12 James declares: 'Blessed is the man who perseveres under trial, because when he has stood the test, he will receive the crown of life that God has promised to those who love him.' Just as he did in his earlier discussion of this topic, James here informs us that trials are a means to test our faith. In James 1:2-4, he told us how 'trials of many kinds' are used to test us. There he had in mind a vast array of external challenges such as physical suffering and persecution. Here, however, James has one very specific type of trial in mind — the trial of our temptations.[1] In James 1:12-18, James reminds us that, like my bar exam, the Christian life is an arduous test involving a continual struggle with temptation. But James also assures us that through our union with Jesus Christ, we can triumph even in the test of our temptations.

## The source of our temptations

The first thing James reveals to us about our temptations is their source. James makes it absolutely clear that our temptations do not come from God, 'When tempted, no one should say, "God is tempting me." For God cannot be tempted by evil, nor does he tempt anyone,' (James 1:13). While God is the source of other forms of trials, such as those emphasized in James 1:2-4, he is not the source of the trial of our temptations.[2]

So if God is not the source, then who is? In a couple of places James indicates that our great adversary, the devil, has some role in tempting us. For example, in 4:7 James declares: 'Submit yourselves, then, to God. *Resist the devil*, and he will flee from you' (emphasis mine). Clearly, James considers the devil as a source of our temptations.

However, while the devil is *a* source of temptation, James does not see the devil as the *main* source of our temptations. James identifies the main source of our temptations in James 1:14: 'but each one is tempted when, *by his own* evil desire, he is dragged away and enticed,' (emphasis mine). According to James, *we* are the source of our temptations. We give ourselves this test. In other words, James tells us that we have seen the enemy and it is us. As Peter Davids puts it: 'God does not test you ... rather you test yourself!'[3]

James totally insulates God from any involvement with our internal temptations with sin. God is pure and holy. He cannot have any fellowship with darkness. In addition, God does not play spiritual games with us. He does not entice us to sin. We are solely to blame for our temptations and sin. We are the source of our temptations.

After revealing this to us, James proceeds to tell us what will happen when our temptations are allowed to go unchecked. He shows us the results of our failure to pass the test. In James 1:14-15, James unfolds for us the life-cycle of sin.


## The life-cycle of sin

I was a very poor science student. Frankly, I don't remember very much from my science classes. However, one thing I do recall is the unit on the life-cycle of a frog. I remember this unit so well because it involved leaving the classroom and taking a trip to the river behind our school. There we captured some tadpoles and put them into an aquarium. The purpose of this experiment was to witness the life-cycle of a frog, but, like many primary school science projects, things went awry. Unfortunately, the life-cycle of the tadpoles was cut short!

Although the tadpoles came to an untimely demise, the point of the unit was not lost on me. I learned that there were three stages in the life-cycle of a frog. A frog's life begins in egg form. After the egg hatches, a tadpole emerges. The tadpole, in turn, develops legs and finally becomes the amphibious creature we know as a frog. James tells us that there are also three main stages in the life-cycle of sin — desire, deeds and death.

*Desire*

The first stage in the life-cycle of sin is our own internal evil desire. Note James' words in James 1:14: 'but each one is tempted when, *by his own evil desire*, he is dragged away and enticed,' (emphasis mine). James tells us that sinful deeds have their genesis in our own inner thought life. Sin is conceived in our hearts and minds. The Greek word translated as 'desire' in James 1:14 means to possess a lustful unrestrained craving for something forbidden. It is this type of misdirected desire that sends us down the pathway to fully-fledged sin. James tells us that when we fail to nip our evil desires in the bud we are doomed to be 'dragged away' and 'enticed' by them.

The Greek words translated as 'dragged away' and 'enticed' are very revealing words. They both come from the world of hunting and fishing. The Greek word behind the phrase 'dragged away' refers to the process of catching a fish. The image is of a fish which is enticed to grasp a baited hook and then is caught and dragged out of the water. The Greek word translated as 'enticed' refers to the action of a hunter who lures his prey into a trap by enticing it with alluring bait.[4]

Note what James is telling us through these two words. He is telling us that when it comes to sin we are both the hunter and the prey. He tells us that we are our own worst enemy. We set our own hook and bait ourselves into our own traps. We allow our own evil desires to overtake us. This is the first stage in the life-cycle of sin.

*Deeds*

The next stage in the life-cycle of sin occurs when our evil desires are not snuffed out in the thought stage. In James 1:15, James informs us that unfettered evil desires eventually give birth to evil deeds: 'Then, after desire has conceived, it gives birth to sin.' As one commentator bluntly put it: 'Lust is the mother of sin.'[5] Sinful deeds represent the second stage in the life-cycle of sin.

*Death*

In James 1:15, James indicates that death is the culminating stage of the life-cycle of sin: 'Then, after desire has conceived, it gives birth to sin; and sin, when it is full-grown, *gives birth to death*,' (emphasis mine). Like Paul, James reminds us of the horrific truth that the wages of sin is death (Romans 6:23). Sin brings both physical and spiritual death.

Thus James shows us that the life-cycle of sin begins with the conception of evil desires in our hearts. These evil desires then give birth to sinful action in our lives. Finally, these sinful deeds bring death and destruction. This is the nature of the dreadful life-cycle of sin.

## The example of Amnon

The Bible provides us with many examples of how this life-cycle unfolds in real life. One such example can be found in 2 Samuel 13 and involves King David's eldest son Amnon. Amnon had become infatuated with his half-sister Tamar. The Bible states that he 'fell in love' with Tamar (2 Samuel 13:1) and quickly became 'frustrated' by his inability to have sexual relations with her (2 Samuel 13:2). Amnon's evil desire represents the first stage of the life-cycle of sin.

Amnon entered into stage two of the life-cycle of sin when his evil desire gave birth to evil deeds. This occurred when Amnon entered into a conspiracy with his friend Jonadab to lure Tamar into his house by feigning sickness. After Tamar arrived at the house with some food for her allegedly sick half-brother, Amnon demanded that everyone leave the house except for Tamar. When he had her alone, Amnon then lured Tamar into his bedroom: 'Then Amnon said to Tamar, "Bring the food here into my bedroom so that I may eat from your hand,"' (2 Samuel 13:10). It was at this moment that his lustful thoughts gave birth to a fully-fledged sinful deed: 'But when she took it to him to eat, he grabbed her and said, "Come to bed with me, my sister,"' (2 Samuel 13:11). Amnon raped Tamar.[6]

Amnon's sad story did not end with his sinful deed. He moved to stage three. When Amnon's brother, Absalom, learned of the rape of Tamar he plotted to kill Amnon and eventually carried out his plot (2 Samuel 13:28-29). The end result of Amnon's lustful desires and sinful deeds was death. Amnon's sin not only placed him in peril of spiritual death, but it also led to his physical death as well.

Clearly, Amnon failed the test of his temptation. He baited his own hook with lustful thoughts about Tamar and he was dragged away into sin and, eventually, into death. How many times have you lived out this life-cycle of sin? How many times have you failed the test of your temptations? How many times have you allowed your thought life to drift into coveting the forbidden? How many times have you allowed an unchecked desire to bloom into a sinful deed? Remember the ramifications of failing the test of our temptations. The stakes are incredibly high. The consequences are eternal. Don't forget James' warning that sin 'gives birth to death' (James 1:15).

After hearing these stern words of warning about the consequences of failing the test of our temptations it would be easy for us to become discouraged. After all, we all recognize how easily we are baited into sin by our own evil desires. It seems as though we are doomed to death. We all seem destined to experience the fate of Amnon. Given this reality, how can any of us hope to avoid the life-cycle of sin? How can we possibly hope to pass the test of our temptations? This brings us to our final topic — the source of our triumph.

## The source of our triumph

James assures us that we can indeed triumph over our temptations. He reveals to us that, while God is not the source of our temptations, he is the source of our triumph over those temptations. James tells us that in order to pass the test of our temptations we must look to God who is the source of every good gift: 'Every good and perfect gift is from above, coming down from the Father of the heavenly lights, who does not change like shifting shadows,' (James 1:17). God does not give us temptations, but rather he sends us heavenly gifts which help us to triumph over our temptations. Of course, the greatest of all these heavenly gifts is God's own dear Son, the Lord Jesus Christ (John 3:16). James informs us that our victory is found in the heavenly gift of Jesus Christ.

James makes an indirect reference to the gift of Jesus in the language and imagery he employs in James 1:18. In this verse, James declares that it was God who 'chose to give us birth through the word of truth, that we might be a kind of firstfruits of all he created'. Here James tells us that while our own sinful thoughts give birth to sin, God's heavenly gift to us gives birth to a new creation 'through the word of truth'. Jesus is the 'word of truth'. He is both the Word of God (John 1:1) and the truth (John 14:6). Furthermore, it is Jesus who allows us to experience a new birth and to become new creations: 'Therefore, if anyone is in Christ, he is a new creation; the old has gone, the new has come!' (2 Corinthians 5:17). It is only through the heavenly gift of Jesus Christ that we are able to triumph over our temptations. It is only through the work of Jesus Christ that we can become the 'firstfruits' of all God has created (James 1:18).

## Firstfruits

James' use of the term 'firstfruits' in reference to us should bring us tremendous encouragement. This word is rife with glorious meaning. In the Old Testament, the concept of firstfruits had a three-fold meaning. First, it reminded the people that God owns everything. The entire harvest was his. Second, it reminded them that God expected his people to give him their best. The firstfruits were the best part of the harvest and God called on his people to offer this part of the harvest to him. Finally, and most importantly, the firstfruits were a reminder of God's faithfulness in providing for his people. James uses this Old Testament imagery of the firstfruits and applies it to us. He tells us that *we* are God's firstfruits.

The fact that we are considered God's firstfruits reveals two very powerful truths to us about our destiny. First, it reminds us that God owns our entire lives. We are his. He controls our destiny. Second, it also informs us that we represent the best part of the harvest of his creation, we are the 'firstfruits *of all he created*' (James 1:18, emphasis mine). In other words, God considers us as his crowning creative achievement.

Because we are considered God's firstfruits we know with certainty that God will not leave the work of his hands. He will produce a spiritual harvest of holiness in us. We will be the 'firstfruits of all he created'. It is guaranteed to happen because God has decreed it. As Paul states in Philippians 1:6, he who began a good work in us 'will carry it on to completion until the day of Christ Jesus'. Daniel Doriani summarizes the assurance which is found in the reality that we are God's firstfruits:

James says God's people are his firstfruits. We are the first and the best of his 'produce'. He will prove faithful. He will care for us year by year, even as he cared for Israel in the wilderness. This is what the tests should teach us. If we fail, our failure teaches us to turn to God for mercy, as he offers it in the gospel. Then as we persevere with him in love, come what may, we will receive the crown of life that he has promised.[7]

The concept of the firstfruits assures us that we will ultimately triumph over our temptations. God is the source of our triumph.

## Tempted in every way

I began this chapter by describing the gruelling nature of my bar exam. I noted that one of the most difficult aspects of that exam was that I spent five months waiting to learn if I passed. I spent five months just dangling in the wind, unsure of whether I would triumph. Then the letter finally came. I remember running upstairs into my bedroom and kneeling in prayer over that envelope prior to opening it. I also recall with amazing clarity the adulation for God that came over me as I learned that I had passed the test.

One of the most comforting truths found in this passage is that it reveals to us that we never have to experience this type of limbo in the Christian life. God does not leave us hanging in self-doubt about whether we will receive the crown of life. Instead he assures us that we have already passed the test because Jesus has passed the test for us.

In James 1:12, James declares: 'Blessed is the man who perseveres under trial, because when he has stood the test, he will receive the crown of life that God has promised to those who love him.' Jesus is the blessed man of whom James speaks in this verse. He is the one who has stood the test for us. He is the one who has earned the crown of life for us. Jesus is the Word that has given us new birth. Jesus is the true firstfruits (1 Corinthians 15:20). Jesus has passed the test of our temptations for us. As the writer to the Hebrews so properly reminds us: 'For we do not have a high priest who is unable to sympathize with our weaknesses, *but we have one who has been tempted in every way, just as we are — yet was without sin*' (Hebrews 4:15, emphasis mine). The reality that Jesus has passed the test for us reveals to us how we should deal with our sin when it overtakes us. It reminds us that we must go to Jesus.

James takes up this point again later in his epistle. In James 4:1-5, he chastises his flock for a variety of sinful behaviours including fighting, quarrelling and coveting. After convicting them of their sin, he then graciously reveals to them the remedy for their sin. He tells them that even when they fail the test by allowing their evil desires to flower into evil deeds, all is not lost. In James 4:6-10, he tells his flock that God's grace is great enough to cover even their worst sins:

> But he gives us more grace. That is why Scripture says: 'God opposes the proud but gives grace to the humble.' Submit yourselves, then, to God. Resist the devil, and he will flee from you. Come near to God and he will come near to you. Wash your hands, you sinners, and purify your hearts, you double-minded. Grieve, mourn and wail. Change your laughter to mourning and your joy to gloom. Humble yourselves before the Lord, and he will lift you up.

If you come near to Christ, and humble yourself before him, he will lift you up. In order to triumph in the test of your temptations you must wholeheartedly embrace the one who has passed the test for you.

# 9.

# Responding to the Word:
# hearing and doing

*'My dear brothers, take note of this: Everyone should be quick*
*to listen, slow to speak and slow to become angry, for man's*
*anger does not bring about the righteous life that God desires.*
*Therefore, get rid of all moral filth and the evil that is so*
*prevalent, and humbly accept the word planted in you, which*
*can save you. Do not merely listen to the word, and so deceive*
*yourselves. Do what it says'*
(James 1:19-22).

'Just Do It.' Those three words served as the centrepiece of one of the most successful corporate advertising campaigns in history. The 'Just Do It' slogan revived the once floundering brand of Nike Corporation. Nike used this ad campaign to convince average people that they too could accomplish great athletic feats like those performed by basketball player Michael Jordan and golfer Tiger Woods. Nike convinced people that all they had to do was spend some of their hard earned cash on a pair of Nike training shoes and then they too could 'Just Do It.'

Nike's 'Just Do It' slogan obviously stresses the importance of taking action. After all, successful athletes do not simply think about their sport, they *do* their sport. While Tiger Woods may be a student of golf strategy and technique, he is famous because he actually goes out on the golf course and 'does' golf. Action is vital in sport. It is also vital in the Christian life.

In some sense, James conceives of the Christian life as an athletic performance. Like a good athlete, James expects us to perform in the Christian life. He is not content with merely cerebral Christians who can recite Bible verses, but who fail to live out God's Word. Instead, James calls Christians to 'Just Do It': he calls them to live out the Bible, to 'just do' the Word. In this chapter, we'll learn how to respond properly to the Word of God. James tells us that responding to God's Word involves two steps: hearing the Word; and, most importantly, doing the Word.

## Hearing the Word

James begins this section of his epistle in a Proverbs-like manner. Like the sage of Proverbs, James calls his readers to listen rather than speak: 'My dear brothers, take note of this: *Everyone should be quick to listen, slow to speak* and slow to become angry,' (James 1:19, emphasis mine). In this verse James introduces the topic of controlling our speech. This is a major theme of his epistle, one which he explores in greater detail in James 3:1-12. James is very concerned about the potentially devastating consequences that can flow from an unbridled tongue. Here, however, James is not so much concerned with the destructive aspects of speech as he is with the destructive aspects of failing to listen. In other words, James' main emphasis here is on the importance of listening, particularly listening to God's Word.

That James is emphasizing the importance of listening to God's Word is evidenced by the verses which precede and follow James 1:19. In these verses James emphasizes the Word. For example, note James 1:18: 'He chose to give us birth through the *word of truth*,' (emphasis mine). James 1:21-23 contain a similar emphasis:

James 1:21:  'Therefore, get rid of all moral filth and the evil that is so prevalent, and humbly accept the *word* planted in you, which can save you,' (emphasis mine).

James 1:22:  'Do not merely *listen to the word*, and so deceive yourselves. Do what it says,' (emphasis mine).

James 1:23:  'Anyone who *listens to the word* but does not do what it says is like a man who looks at his face in a mirror,' (emphasis mine).

Clearly, James' focus in this section is on listening to the Word of God. He is admonishing us to be hearers of the Word.

The reason that James emphasizes so passionately the importance of hearing the Word is because he knows that growth in the Christian life requires the power of the Word. While God has revealed himself in other ways, such as in his creation, it is his written Word that speaks most profoundly about his attributes, nature and plan for us and this world. If you want to grow in the Christian life you must feed on the nutritious nectar of God's Word, and in order to feed on God's Word you must first hear it. Simply put, living the Christian life is only possible when we listen to God as he speaks to us in his Word.

So where does God speak to us in his Word? In one sense, we hear God speaking through his Word every time we open the Bible and read it. This is why all Christians should engage in some form of regular personal Bible reading.[1] However, while personal Bible reading is important, the primary place we hear God speaking to us through his Word is through preaching. God speaks to you through the Word as it is preached. The question is: 'Are you listening?'

Most Christians have heard hundreds of sermons and, whether they will admit it or not, every time the preacher enters the pulpit they are critiquing his work. Most Christians have become experts on evaluating the delivery of sermons. However, very few Christians have spent much time assessing whether they are good recipients of sermons. While pastors spend years learning how to preach a sermon, Christians generally spend precious little time learning how to listen to one. Have you ever asked yourself, 'Am I a good listener to the Word of God? Am I really listening to the word preached? Am I hearing the word?'

When I was in seminary, I was required to preach numerous times in our seminary chapel. After preaching, I was graded by my fellow students according to a list of objective criteria. This was often a painful and embarrassing process, but it helped me to become a better preacher. It was important for me to evaluate my skills in the pulpit. I think listeners of the Word should evaluate their listening skills by also using a list of objective criteria. All Christians should give themselves a hearing test to determine if they are truly hearing the Word preached. Where can we find such a set of criteria by which to test whether we are good listeners? A good place to start is question 160 of the *Westminster Larger Catechism*: 'What is required of those that hear the word preached?'

> It is required of those that hear the word preached, that they attend upon it with diligence, preparation, and prayer; examine what they hear by the scriptures; receive the truth with faith, love, meekness, and readiness of mind, as the word of God; meditate, and confer of it; hide it in their hearts, and bring forth the fruit of it in their lives.

Here the catechism gives us three basic criteria by which we can evaluate our listening. It outlines for us what it takes to become a good hearer of the Word. According to the catechism a good hearer of the Word prepares, prays and ponders. Let's look at each of these criteria in more detail.

*Preparation*

If we accept that the preaching of the Word is the primary way in which God speaks to us then it follows that we should come to church prepared to listen to it. How can we prepare ourselves to listen to preaching? One simple way to prepare is by coming to church sufficiently rested. That means we must go to sleep at a reasonable hour on Saturday night. Another way to prepare to listen to the Word is by consciously emptying our minds of all worldly concerns as we listen to the sermon. Do you come prepared to listen to the Word?

*Prayer*

All Christians should pray in advance for the preaching of the Word. During the week, and particularly on Saturday night and Sunday morning, you should pray both for the minister, that he may preach with the blessing of the Spirit, and for yourself, that you may receive the Word and have it applied by the Spirit to your own heart and mind. Prayer is vital to becoming a better hearer of the Word. Do you pray regularly for these things?

*Pondering the Word*

Our hearing of the Word does not stop after the preacher closes his sermon on Sunday morning. We are called to continue to hear the Word by pondering it throughout the week. Sometimes we actually hear the Word most powerfully, not on Sunday, but during the week as we mull over and meditate on Sunday's sermon. It is amazing how many times the preached Word will find relevant application in your life if you keep pondering during the week. A good way to ponder the Word throughout the week is by re-reading and reviewing the sermon text, sermon outline and your sermon notes in your personal devotions. Pondering the Word allows us to continue to hear God speaking to us all week long. Do you ponder the Word preached?

James informs us that the first way we are to properly respond to God's Word is by hearing it. However, becoming a good hearer of the Word is only the first step. James demands much more of us. He demands that we also become *doers* of the Word.

## Doing the Word

We live in the 'information' age. The average citizen of the twenty-first century is bombarded daily with thousands of titbits of information. We receive information from television, newspapers, magazines and the Internet. However, while we live in an information-saturated world, it often seems like we employ very little of this knowledge in our actual lives. There seems to be a vast disconnection between information and action. We have become consumers of information rather than users of information. We have become passive learners. We *hear* much, but we *do* little.

The twenty-first-century church has not been left unscathed by this cultural phenomenon. The church has never had more access to the Word of God. Preaching is available '24/7' through a variety of media. However, this increased access to the Word has not led to increased action in our lives. We hear much, but we do little. We have become passive learners in the pew. We have become 'pew potatoes', the church equivalent of 'couch potatoes'. We *hear* the Word, but we fail to *do* the Word.

James will simply not tolerate such a dichotomy in our lives. He will not allow us to be passive hearers of the Word. Note what he says in James 1:23-24: 'Anyone who listens to the word *but does not do what it says* is like a man who looks at his face in a mirror and, after looking at himself, goes away and immediately forgets what he looks like,' (emphasis mine). Do you see what James is saying here? He is saying that listening is not enough. A Christian must also actually *do* what the Word says.

James will not permit us to pat ourselves on the back and say, 'What a good Christian I am! I have done my devotions all week and listened attentively to the sermon on Sunday.' As commentator J. A. Motyer notes, James would respond to such a declaration in this way:

> Well done! But now, what about obeying the word you read? Have you actually changed your mind so that you now hold to be true what you learnt in the word? Have you (and are you) re-directing your imagination and your eyes and your thoughts so as to live according to the standards of the word? Are your relationships different, as the word instructed you they should be?[2]

According to James, hearing the Word is simply not enough, we must also put the Word into action — we must be doers of the Word.

The reason James is so adamant about the necessity of doing the Word is because he considers the doing of the Word as evidence of our faith in God and, more importantly, as evidence of God's work in us. In other words, James views the doing of the Word as an objective measuring stick to judge the validity of our faith. This is a biblical idea. When God sends forth his Word it does not return void, it accomplishes its purpose (Isaiah 55:11). The Word of God, when it is received in true faith, changes people and their behaviour. It produces concrete and measurable results. It does something in and through us. When we do what the Word says, we demonstrate our faith and commitment to Christ.

Unfortunately, many Christians hear the Word but fail to carry it out. They seem to accept the Word in principle, but reject it in practice. When this occurs, there is no genuine growth in the Christian life. When we fail to put the Word into practice we end up unchanged by its power.

James explains this dynamic through his illustration of the man in the mirror: 'Anyone who listens to the word but does not do what it says is like a man who looks at his face in a mirror and, after looking at himself, goes away and immediately forgets what he looks like,' (James 1:23-24). In these verses James compares the man who hears the Word but fails to do it to a man who looks at his face in a mirror, leaves the mirror and then immediately forgets what he looks like. In the illustration the mirror is the Word of God. Like the Word of God, a mirror has a revelatory function — mirrors allow us to see ourselves. When we fail to do something about what the mirror of God's Word reveals to us it becomes worthless. Let me explain this with my own illustration involving a mirror.

Have you ever had lunch with someone and then you go to the bathroom, look into the mirror and are aghast because the mirror reveals to you that you have a big piece of lettuce stuck between two of your teeth? This is an awful feeling. As you were eating you were entirely unaware of this major flaw in your appearance, but the mirror revealed it to you.

Now what do you do when you become aware of the fact that you have lettuce between your teeth? Do you walk away and forget about it? Of course not! That would be silly. But that's exactly what we do when we hear the Word and fail to act upon it. Like a mirror, the Word of God enables us to see all of our flaws and calls us to take immediate remedial action. When we hear the Word and fail to do it we are like the man who looks in the mirror for a moment and walks away leaving the lettuce between his teeth. A person who merely hears the Word and then forgets it remains unchanged and unaffected by the Word of God. Such a person does not grow in the Christian life. This is why doing the Word is so essential. It leads to growth and change.

According to James, it is only the doer of the Word who receives God's blessing: 'But the man who looks intently into the perfect law that gives freedom, and continues to do this, not forgetting what he has heard, *but doing it — he will be blessed in what he does,*' (James 1:25, emphasis mine). Unlike the man who looks into the mirror and forgets what he looks like, this man 'continues' to remember his image, he does not forget what he has heard, but even more importantly this second man does something about it: he takes action regarding what he sees. This man not only hears the Word, but he also does the Word and because he is a doer of the Word he is 'blessed in what he does'.

James concludes this section of his epistle by reminding us once again that it is the doer of the Word who pleases God. Note James' definition of religion that God accepts: 'Religion that God our Father accepts as pure and faultless is this: to look after orphans and widows in their distress and to keep oneself from being polluted by the world,' (James 1:27). When James defines religion that God finds both 'pure' and 'faultless' he does *not* say, 'Religion that God our Father accepts as pure and faultless is this: to hear the Word and do nothing about it, to study theology without applying its truth to our lives, and to allow ourselves to be polluted by the world.' Instead James defines the essence of true religion as *doing* the Word by looking after orphans and widows and by keeping ourselves from being polluted by the world. True religion involves both hearing and doing the Word of God. It is only when we hear *and* do the Word that we can live acceptable and pleasing lives before our God. This is how we are to respond to God's Word.

## The parable of the sower [or soils]

James' main point in this part of his letter is abundantly clear. He teaches us that how we respond to the Word of God matters to the Christian life. He tells us many will hear the Word, but few will actually do what it says.

In many ways, James' point here is similar to that of Jesus in the parable of the sower (Mark 4:3-20). James is once again echoing his brother's teaching. In the parable of the sower Jesus informs his disciples that the preached Word of God will meet with a variety of different responses. He does this by comparing the Word of God to seed which is sown upon four different types of soil.

First, there is the soil of the *walking path*. This soil has become hard due to the traffic which crosses it. Accordingly, when the seed falls upon this soil it fails to penetrate it and simply remains on the surface to become food for the birds.

The second type of soil upon which the seed falls is *rocky soil*. Because this soil is so rocky the seed is unable to establish a deep root system; it can penetrate only so far. Yes, the seed begins to grow quickly, but its growth is only temporary because the young plant is quickly scorched by the sun and dies because it lacks a sufficient root system.

The third type of soil is filled with *thorns and weeds*. This soil also permits the seed to grow temporarily, but once again it quickly dies because it is choked by the weeds which grow around it.

Finally, there is the *good soil*. Jesus describes what happens to the seed when it falls on this soil: 'It came up, grew and produced a crop, multiplying thirty, sixty, or even a hundred times,' (Mark 4:8).

These four types of soil represent four possible responses of our heart to God's Word. All four soils were exposed to God's Word, but in only one did it produce lasting fruit. According to

Jesus, the good soil is the one which hears, accepts and *does* the Word. James teaches us the very same principle. The faithful Christian is the Christian who hears the Word, accepts it and then does it. This is the Christian who truly has the Word 'planted' in him, as James notes in James 1:21.

Which type of soil best describes you? How do you respond to God's Word? Does the Word of God take root when it is sown upon your heart or does it fail to penetrate beyond the surface? Does it produce a crop of living righteousness or does it become choked to death by the cares of the world? Are *you* properly responding to God's Word? Are *you* hearing it? Even more importantly, are *you* doing it? Remember, James tells us that it is only the Christian who does the Word who is blessed: 'But the man who looks intently into the perfect law that gives freedom, and continues to do this, not forgetting what he has heard, but doing it — he will be blessed in what he does,' (James 1:25). If you long to be blessed in the Christian life then you must become not only a hearer of God's Word, but a doer of it as well.

# 10.

# The problem of partiality

*'My brothers, as believers in our glorious Lord Jesus Christ,*
*don't show favouritism. Suppose a man comes into your meeting*
*wearing a gold ring and fine clothes, and a poor man in shabby*
*clothes also comes in. If you show special attention to the man*
*wearing fine clothes and say, "Here's a good seat for you," but*
*say to the poor man, "You stand there" or "Sit on the floor by my*
*feet," have you not discriminated among yourselves*
*and become judges with evil thoughts?'*
(James 2:1-4).

On 1 December 1955, a young black seamstress named
Rosa Parks boarded a bus in Montgomery, Alabama. She
took a seat in the section reserved for 'coloured' people. At that
time, the city of Montgomery had an ordinance that mandated
segregated seating on public buses. This ordinance showed
partiality to white people by giving them the front seats of the
bus. Black people were required to sit at the back of the bus.
If the 'white' section of the bus became overcrowded, the bus
driver had the authority to extend this section by evicting black
passengers from their seats and commanding them to move

further back in the bus in order to make room for additional white passengers. This is what happened to Rosa Parks in 1955. Although she rightly took a seat in the 'coloured' section of the bus, the seats set aside for white people became filled and the driver demanded that she give up her seat to a white passenger. In one of the most courageous and famous acts of civil disobedience in American history, Rosa Parks refused to relinquish her seat. She was eventually arrested for violating Montgomery's segregation laws. Her valiant act helped to spark the Civil Rights movement in the United States.

While the Bible calls us to be discriminatory regarding a person's belief and conduct, it is adamant in its condemnation of all forms of discrimination based on a person's race, ethnicity, or socio-economic status. One of the most vivid examples of the Bible's condemnation of these unjustified forms of discrimination can be found in James 2:1-13. Although the members of James' flock were not dealing with the issue of racial discrimination, they were dealing with an equally heinous problem, discrimination based on wealth, appearance and social status. Simply put, James' flock was showing partiality to the wealthy and he severely chastises them for allowing this type of favouritism to be practised in the church. He opens this section by bluntly declaring these words to his flock: 'My brothers, as believers in our glorious Lord Jesus Christ, *don't show favouritism*,' (James 2:1). By issuing this unequivocal prohibition against favouritism, James reminds us that biblically unjustified forms of partiality are entirely inconsistent with the Christian life.

## Partiality portrayed

After issuing his condemnation against partiality in the first verse of this chapter, James proceeds to give his congregation an illustration of the type of behaviour he is condemning. He shows them what sinful partiality looks like. It is possible that James drew this illustration from actual events which had occurred in this congregation or he may have fabricated a fictional account, similar to a parable, in order to illustrate his point. Whatever the origin of this illustration, it is extremely vivid and effective in displaying the type of behaviour that James calls us to avoid. In this illustration we see partiality portrayed.

The illustration James gives us involves two men who enter the church for worship.[1] The first man who enters the church is described by James as wearing a 'gold ring' and 'fine clothes' (2:2). These two pieces of information indicate that this man was very wealthy. We know this because gold rings served as a status symbol for the Roman upper class known as the equestrian class, and the phrase 'fine clothes' indicates that the man's clothing was of a very high quality. In other words, this first man was a wealthy and well-dressed man. He was a man of status and means.

Simultaneous with the entrance of this wealthy man, a second man enters the church. This man is very different from the first. He is clearly *not* wealthy. James describes him as 'a poor man in shabby clothes' (2:2). The word 'shabby' doesn't quite do justice to James' description of this man's clothing. The Greek word which is translated as 'shabby' is the same word which is translated as 'filth' in James 1:21. In other words, this man had a vile appearance and likely broadcasted an equally vile odour.

After introducing these two vastly different men, James then uses them to illustrate the nature of sinful partiality. He does this by suggesting a hypothetical response on the part of the congregation to these two men as they enter the church: 'If you show special attention to the man wearing fine clothes and say, "Here's a good seat for you," but say to the poor man, "You stand there" or "Sit on the floor by my feet," have you not discriminated among yourselves and become judges with evil thoughts?' (2:3-4). Do you see how this hypothetical response displays sinful partiality on the part of the church? The wealthy man is shown partiality by being immediately escorted to a prominent seat in the church while the poor man is unjustly discriminated against by being denied a seat; instead he is required to stand at the back of the church or sit on the floor. James condemns this blatant and unjust display of partiality. He will not tolerate Christians making value judgements about other people based on illegitimate criteria like wealth and social status. James refers to such unjust judgements as flowing from 'evil thoughts' (2:4).

## This is our problem

Now when we first encounter James' illustration of partiality we might be tempted to dismiss it as irrelevant to the modern church context. It would be easy to consider it as a sad commentary on the problems of the early church. We might want to say in response to this illustration, 'I am so glad the church no longer has this problem.' Of course, such a response would be incorrect. While James' illustration of partiality may be outdated, it is by no means irrelevant to the church today. The very situation James describes in this illustration can, and does, happen in the modern church. Consider, for example, the following updated version of James' illustration and as you consider it ask yourself: 'Could this scenario occur in my church?'

*A modern version of James' illustration*

It is Easter morning and the church is packed to capacity. The ushers are scurrying about, setting up folding chairs in the overflow section of the church. Then in walks Mr Gates. He is a bit late for worship, as he usually is, because he likes to park his Lexus in a distant part of the car park to avoid anyone damaging it. Mr Gates enters the church emanating the aroma of fine cologne and he is dressed in an exquisitely tailored Italian suit. One of the ushers immediately recognizes him and rushes up to greet him. 'Good morning, Mr Gates!' he exclaims. He then informs Mr Gates that he has reserved for him a fine seat in the first pew. The usher escorts him there and with a warm grin declares, 'Here's a good seat for you.' The usher is very pleased with the service he has rendered to the influential Mr Gates. After all, as everyone in the church knows, Mr Gates' tithe accounts for nearly one quarter of the church's annual budget.

After patting himself on the back, the usher's attention is quickly diverted by a chaotic situation developing at the back of the church. He sees that some people are leaving the church and others are trying to move to other seats. At first the usher cannot identify the source of the chaos, but then his nostrils are assaulted by an unpleasant odour and his nose quickly connects this to a man who has taken a seat in the overflow section of the church. The usher grimaces because he recognizes this man as an annoying beggar who frequently shows up on the church's doorstep asking for money. After releasing a heavy sigh, the usher rushes up to this man and demands that he give up his seat. The usher then escorts the man to a room in the basement of the church, which receives an audio feed of the worship service, and declares to the man, in a condescending tone, 'I am sure you will be more comfortable here.'

This scenario could occur in any modern affluent congregation on any given Sunday. The problem James describes is neither ancient nor irrelevant, but rather it is a problem with which we continue to grapple. The problem of partiality continues to plague the church. It is *our* problem. I know this because I have personally engaged in this type of sinful behaviour. Let me share with you one overt case of sinful partiality from my own life which closely parallels the illustration given to us by James.

During an evening worship service of a church I was serving, a man walked in about halfway through the service. Like the man in James' illustration, this man was wearing shabby clothes and reeked of alcohol and cigarettes. He took a seat in the pew directly in front of my wife and family. I responded to this man with immediate suspicion. I was distracted during the entire worship service because I was keeping an eye on this man's every movement. I assumed the worst about him. However, I know that if that very same man had entered our church wearing a suit and tie my reaction would have been entirely different. I would have assumed the best of him. I would have greeted him warmly. I would probably have extended hospitality to him. I would have shown him partiality.

Now perhaps you have never engaged in such an overt form of the sin of partiality, but my guess is that you have nonetheless frequently engaged in some form of this sin. There are many subtle ways to engage in the sin of partiality. For instance, some churches engage in this sin is by making wealthy and educated people officers of the church, not because they necessarily have the biblical qualifications for such positions, but simply because they give the church a lot of money or because they are considered successful by the standards of the world. Another even more subtle way that we display partiality is by consciously avoiding certain people in the church that we categorize as 'undesirable'. The problem of partiality is indeed our problem and, as James goes on to explain, it is a very serious problem in the eyes of God.

## Partiality condemned

After portraying the nature of partiality, James next explains why it is worthy of condemnation. In James 2:5-13, he informs us that when we practise partiality we act contrary to both God's character and his commands.

# The problem of partiality

## *Contrary to God's character*

In order to understand why practising partiality is contrary to the character of God we must first understand the literal meaning of the Greek word which is translated as 'favouritism' in this section of James' epistle. This Greek word literally means to 'receive the face'. Thus, according to James, when we engage in partiality, or favouritism, we are committing the error of judging people based solely on their external appearance. In other words, partiality involves judging a book by its cover, rather than by its substance. It involves rendering a judgement based on superficial criteria. This is what James' flock was doing with the rich among them. These rich people may have looked good on the outside, but James reminds them that it was these well-dressed individuals who were 'exploiting' them, 'dragging' them into court and 'slandering' the name of Jesus (2:6-7). God viewed them from an entirely different perspective. He never renders a judgement based on superficial criteria. He never 'receives the face', but rather he looks at the heart. God's perfect and holy character simply will not allow him to favour someone based on illegitimate grounds. This aspect of God's character is most powerfully displayed for us in the life of our Lord Jesus Christ.

During his earthly ministry, Jesus always judged people by the spiritual status of their heart. He never showed partiality to a people because they were socially significant or wealthy. He never pandered to the wealthy. He never discriminated against the poor. Instead, like his Father, Jesus displayed a godly form of partiality by favouring those who were considered socially insignificant. Think back to James' illustration and ask yourself, 'Which of the two men in James' illustration would Jesus have favoured?' The answer is obvious. Jesus would have shown partiality to the poor man in shabby clothes.

An essential part of God's character is that he displays mercy to those who are in need. James reminds his flock, and us, that we are recipients of this divine mercy. In James 2:5, he tells his flock they were all spiritually poor and shabby and yet God had shown favour to them by granting them salvation: 'Listen, my dear brothers: Has not God chosen those who are poor in the eyes of the world to be rich in faith and to inherit the kingdom he promised those who love him?' God shows partiality and mercy to the poor. He cares for the widow, the orphan and the foreigner. Thus when we show partiality to the rich and discriminate against the poor we are acting contrary to the character of God.

*Contrary to God's commands*

However, engaging in the type of partiality condemned by James is not only a violation of God's character, but it is also a violation of God's commands. In James 2:8-9, James tells us that partiality is contrary to God's law: 'If you really keep the *royal law* found in Scripture, "Love your neighbour as yourself," you are doing right. *But if you show favouritism, you sin and are convicted by the law as lawbreakers*' (emphasis mine). Here James describes partiality, or favouritism, as a violation of God's 'royal law'. He tells us that partiality represents a direct transgression of one of the two great commandments, 'Love your neighbour as yourself.' He also informs us that when we practise partiality we 'sin' and we are 'convicted by the law as lawbreakers'. By using such stern and unequivocal language, James leaves no doubt that the partiality he is condemning represents a violation of God's holy and royal law.

Now at this juncture one would think that James has sufficiently proven his point regarding the serious nature of the sin of partiality, but he has more to say on this topic. He wants us to see that partiality is no minor violation of God's law, but rather that it represents a grievous infraction worthy of eternal condemnation. Pastor James understood human nature and he anticipated that his hearers would be tempted to rationalize the sin of partiality by convincing themselves that while partiality may be 'technically' a violation of God's law, it really represents only a minor infraction. James understood our natural inclination to rank our transgressions. He understood that while we might agree that partiality is sinful, we would also contend that it is not *as* sinful as other sins. Don't you sometimes engage in this type of thinking? Humans are always creating their own hierarchy of sins. James knew that his hearers would be inclined to place partiality low on their hierarchy of sins and so in James 2:10-11 he proceeds to counter this inclination by convincing his flock of the severity of the sin of partiality. He does this in two ways.

## Partiality violates the whole law

First, in James 2:10, James informs his flock that when they commit the seeming small sin of partiality they are in fact breaking the entire law of God: 'For whoever keeps the whole law and yet stumbles *at just one point* is guilty of breaking all of it,' (emphasis mine). James will not allow his flock to construct false hierarchies of sin. He tells them that the sin of partiality represents a transgression of the *entire* ('all of it') law of God.[2] According to James, the sin of partiality is no light matter. Rather, it is an integral part of the unified chain of God's law.

## Partiality is murder

In James 2:11, James demonstrates the seriousness and severity of the sin of partiality in a second way — he equates it with murder.

Like his brother Jesus, James understands any form of hatred or anger expressed towards a brother as a form of murder. In the Sermon on the Mount Jesus declared: 'You have heard that it was said to the people long ago, "Do not murder, and anyone who murders will be subject to judgement." But I tell you that anyone who is angry with his brother will be subject to judgement,' (Matthew 5:21-22). According to Jesus, hatred towards one's brother is a form of murder. James views favouritism as a form of hatred towards our brother and thus a form of murder. This connection is made implicitly in James 2:11: 'For he who said, "Do not commit adultery," also said, "Do not murder." If you do not commit adultery *but do commit murder*, you have become a lawbreaker' (emphasis mine). Many commentators suggest that James' words in this verse were specifically targeted at a group of people in his flock who boasted in their sexual purity while blatantly participating in sinful acts of partiality. It is suggested that this group considered adultery as a serious sin, but did not view partiality in the same way. James destroys their thinking by telling them that while they may not have committed adultery, they have committed the equally wicked sin of murder through their acts of sinful partiality.

Clearly, James views partiality as a serious sin. According to James, partiality is no minor offence, but rather it represents a major moral transgression. It violates both God's character and his commands. It represents a violation of God's entire royal law and it is comparable to murder. This is how James views the sin of partiality. More importantly, this is how *God* views the sin of partiality. Is this how you view it?

## Partiality pardoned

Perhaps at this point you are feeling the weight of conviction regarding your own participation in this sin. James wants you to feel this weight; he wants you to think about the seriousness of this sin and the judgement that is reserved for those who fail to repent of it. Note how James emphasizes judgement as he concludes this section: 'Speak and act as those who are going to be judged by the law that gives freedom, because judgement without mercy will be shown to anyone who has not been merciful,' (James 2:12-13). It is proper for us to consider God's judgement for the unmerciful ways in which we have acted by engaging in sinful forms of partiality.

But there is also good news mingled among these words of judgement. Yes, we are indeed guilty of the sin of partiality and thus also guilty of violating the whole royal law of God. Yes, we rightly deserve God's judgement because by engaging in sinful partiality we have failed to show mercy to others. But James also reminds us that God remains merciful even when we are void of mercy. James encourages us with the good news that there is forgiveness in Christ even for a sin as heinous as this. He gives us this good news in the final words of James 2:13 where, after warning us of judgement, he reminds us that 'Mercy triumphs over judgement!' In this tiny four-word sentence, James gives us one of his most direct declarations of the gospel of Jesus Christ. Here he assures us that, through Jesus Christ, mercy will triumph over judgement. For in the cross of Christ, we the shabby and the poor, we who deserved judgement, found mercy instead. That mercy found in the work of Christ can deliver us even from this serious sin. Our calling is to respond to this good news with gratitude. Our calling is to go forth like our Lord and love our neighbours as ourselves. Our calling is to put to death the sin of partiality both in the church and in all aspects of the Christian life.

# 11.
# Faith at work

*'What good is it, my brothers, if a man claims to have faith but
has no deeds? Can such faith save him? Suppose a brother or
sister is without clothes and daily food. If one of you says to him,
"Go, I wish you well; keep warm and well fed," but does nothing
about his physical needs, what good is it? In the same way,
faith by itself, if it is not accompanied by action, is dead. But
someone will say, "You have faith; I have deeds." Show me your
faith without deeds, and I will show you my faith by what I do'*
(James 2:14-18).

There were many issues which sparked the Protestant
Reformation in 1517. One of these issues was the
relationship between faith and works. The importance of this
issue to the Reformation debate is reflected in the fact that one
of the *'solas'* of the Reformation was *sola fide* — by faith alone.[1]
The Reformers were zealous to articulate and defend the biblical
truth that our salvation is not dependent upon *our* works and
*our* righteousness, but rather upon *Christ's* works and *his*
righteousness, which are imputed to the believer through the
gift of faith. The Reformation recaptured the biblical doctrine of

justification by faith alone which is summarized by the apostle Paul in his epistle to the Romans: 'For we maintain that a man is justified by faith apart from observing the law,' (3:28). According to the Reformers, faith is the sole instrument of our salvation. We are saved by faith, and not by our works.

Because of the Reformation's emphasis on faith alone, many Protestants have struggled to make sense of James' arguments found in James 2:14-26. In this section of his epistle, James seems to launch into a fierce polemic against those who would suggest that faith alone — that is, faith unaccompanied by works — is sufficient for salvation. For example, consider James 2:24: 'You see that a person is justified by what he does *and not by faith alone*,' (emphasis mine). James makes a similar statement in James 2:26: 'As the body without the spirit is dead, *so faith without deeds is dead*' (emphasis mine). Because of these statements many scholars have concluded that James is at odds with both the teaching of the Reformers and with the apostle Paul. In fact, it was statements such as these from the epistle of James which led Martin Luther to view this letter with great suspicion and to describe it pejoratively as a 'strawy epistle'.

So, is it true that James is in conflict with the Protestant Reformation and the apostle Paul? Does he in fact teach a doctrine of salvation which requires faith *plus* works? My answer to these two questions is a hearty and emphatic 'No!' In this chapter, we will see that James is not teaching that our salvation is *dependent* on our works, but rather he is teaching that our salvation is *demonstrated* by our works. James is not addressing how we *become* justified, but rather he is addressing how we are to live as those who are *already* justified. In essence, what separates James from Paul is that Paul was dealing with the issue of how one becomes a Christian, and James was dealing with the issue of how one ought to live as a Christian. We can discern that this was James' purpose by examining his audience and his examples.

## His audience

When comparing what Paul and James had to say about faith and works it is vitally important to keep in mind their respective contexts and their intended audiences. For instance, it is important for us to recognize that in those passages in which Paul stressed most vehemently the importance of faith apart from works (i.e. Galatians 3 and Romans 4) he was specifically addressing a group of legalistic Jews, known as 'Judaizers', who were demanding that works of the law were required to be performed as a condition of salvation. In other words, when Paul addressed the relationship between faith and works he was speaking to an audience that was concerned with the issue of how one *becomes* a Christian.

James, on the other hand, wrote his epistle to an entirely different audience. Unlike Paul, James was writing to a group of Jewish Christians who were not struggling with how one becomes a Christian, but rather with how to live faithfully as a Christian in a pagan world. James was speaking to those who had *already* become Christians and who had fallen under the false impression that faith was an entirely intellectual concept requiring no demonstrable change in behaviour.

One way we can discern that James was addressing an audience consisting of those who had already become Christians is simply by reading the opening verse of this section of his epistle. Note how he refers to his audience in James 2:14: 'What good is it, *my brothers*, if a man claims to have faith but has no deeds? Can such faith save him?' (emphasis mine). Here James refers to his audience as 'brothers'. The use of this term indicates that he was speaking to those who shared his commitment to Christ. It reveals that he was speaking to Christians.

A second indication that James was addressing believers is the nature of the hypothetical situation he suggests in James 2:15-17:

Suppose *a brother or sister* is without clothes and daily food. If one of you says to him, 'Go, I wish you well; keep warm and well fed,' but does nothing about his physical needs, what good is it? In the same way, faith by itself, if it is not accompanied by action, is dead [emphasis mine].

This hypothetical scenario assumes an audience of believers. It directly addresses how Christians ought to conduct themselves towards other Christians, towards a 'brother or sister'. This indicates that James was speaking to those who had already become Christians.

This clear difference in context and audience explains the difference in emphases found in Paul and James. Paul was dealing with the issue of how one becomes justified before God. James was dealing with the issue of how one should live after having experienced justification. Paul was confronting the foe of legalism and James was confronting the foe of licence. One commentator summarized the relationship between James and Paul in this manner: 'They are not antagonists facing each other with crossed swords; they stand back to back, confronting different foes of the Gospel.'[2]

## His examples

A second way we can discern that James was addressing the issue of how one ought to live as a Christian rather than how one becomes a Christian is by examining his examples. In this section of his epistle, James uses two diverse Old Testament figures, Abraham and Rahab, as examples to support his argument. The key to understanding the point that James is supporting by these two examples is noticing where he takes us on the timeline of their respective lives.

# Abraham

Abraham is such an obvious choice for James to use in this context. After all, Abraham is a towering figure of faith in the Old Testament and would have been highly regarded by James' primarily Jewish audience. James even plays to his Jewish crowd by referring to Abraham as 'our ancestor' in James 2:21. He understood how powerful and persuasive an example he had in Abraham.

The apostle Paul also recognized the power of the example of Abraham. Paul used Abraham as an example in both Romans and Galatians to demonstrate that faith alone has always been the sole instrument of salvation (see Romans 4:1-18; and Galatians 3:6-18). The life of Abraham demonstrates that salvation is not dependent on works because he was an unbeliever when God called him out of Ur. Abraham performed no works to earn God's favour, he simply responded to the call of the gospel by the gift of faith. Paul appropriately uses Abraham as an example of justification by faith alone because that is exactly how his life as a believer was consummated.

James had no quarrel with Paul's use of Abraham as an example of justification by faith alone. However, James saw another lesson present in the life of Abraham — the need for a living and active faith which manifests itself through good works. James draws this additional lesson by taking us to a different point on the timeline of Abraham's life.

When Paul refers to the faith of Abraham he takes us back to the promises God made to Abraham at his conversion.[3] When Abraham was converted he was given the promise of a male heir and numerous descendants (Genesis 12:1-4). God told Abraham that he would be the father of a nation. By faith alone, Abraham embraced these promises and this was credited to him as righteousness (Genesis 15:6). This is where Paul takes us on the timeline of Abraham's life when he discusses the relationship between faith and works. He takes us back to the beginning of Abraham's faith journey.

James, however, takes us to an event which occurred much later in Abraham's life, well after his conversion. Abraham was required to wait many years for the realization of the promise of a male heir. After he finally realized this promise in the birth of Isaac, God demanded that Abraham perform an incredible work of faith. God commanded Abraham to personally sacrifice Isaac (Genesis 22). It is to this event in Abraham's life that James takes us: 'Was not our ancestor Abraham considered righteous for what he did when *he offered his son Isaac on the altar?*' (James 2:21, emphasis mine).

Why does James focus our attention on this event in Abraham's life? He takes us to this event because it supports his main point. James is trying to assert that the Christian life requires us to perform good works which demonstrate the sincerity and genuineness of our faith. This event in Abraham's life is the preeminent biblical example of demonstrable faith. Long after his conversion, Abraham's faith was tested and proved by his works. This is why God intervened to stay Abraham's hand as he was about to sacrifice Isaac. The angel of the LORD declared to Abraham, 'Do not lay a hand on the boy ... Do not do anything to him. *Now I know that you fear God, because you have not withheld from me your son, your only son,*' (Genesis 22:12, emphasis mine). Abraham demonstrated his faith by his works.

Abraham was not justified by works, but his works served to vindicate and demonstrate the sincerity and reality of his saving faith. James is trying to teach us through this example from Abraham's life that this type of living and active faith must be present in our lives as well. Note the universal conclusion James draws from this episode in Abraham's life: 'You see that a person is justified by what he does and not by faith alone,' (James 2:24).

# Rahab

As we have noted, James' use of Abraham as an example of faith was an obvious one. Abraham is the paramount Old Testament example of a life lived by faith. He possessed all the credentials which would be respected by the first-century Jews to whom James was writing. He was a patriarch. He was the father of Israel. That James would appeal to such a towering figure of faith is certainly not surprising. However, understanding why James chose his second example is a bit more perplexing: 'In the same way, was not even Rahab the prostitute considered righteous for what she did when she gave lodging to the spies and sent them off in a different direction? As the body without the spirit is dead, so faith without deeds is dead,' (James 2:25-26). The second example James uses to support his argument is the shocking example of Rahab.

Why was Rahab such a shocking choice? Just compare her to Abraham. Could there be two more vastly different people than Abraham and Rahab? Abraham was the father of Israel. Rahab was initially an enemy of Israel. Abraham was a patriarch. Rahab was a prostitute. Abraham was a man. Rahab was a woman.[4] Why does James use her as an example? How does she advance and strengthen his argument? Why would James use someone who seems to be the exact opposite of Abraham?

James' use of Rahab is actually a masterful stroke in his argument. James is a good pastor who understands human nature. He knew that one of the risks of using the example of Abraham was that his flock would consider him as such a 'superhero' of the faith that they would conclude that they could never be expected to live like him. In other words, James was concerned that his flock would respond to the example of Abraham's work of faith by saying, 'Well, that was Abraham. He was special. I could never live up to the example of such a great man.' James prevents this reaction by interjecting the example of Rahab.

Just like the great patriarch Abraham, Rahab the prostitute also received the gift of saving faith and then proceeded to demonstrate the sincerity of that faith through works. She first believed in the God of the Hebrews through the witness of the spies who came to stay in her home and then she acted on that faith by preserving their lives and betraying her own city. Just like Abraham, Rahab revealed the vitality and genuineness of her saving faith by her works. Although Abraham and Rahab were very different people, what unites them is that they both demonstrated that they possessed a living and active faith by their works.

The great disparities between Rahab and Abraham actually serve to strengthen James' argument. The example of Rahab allows James to say to his flock, 'Look, *even* a prostitute was able to demonstrate her faith by her works, therefore you have no excuse.' John Calvin commented as follows on James' pairing of Abraham and Rahab:

> He designedly put together two persons so different in their character, in order more clearly to show, that no one, whatever may have been his or her condition, nation, or class in society, has ever been counted righteous without works.[5]

James used the example of Rahab in order to challenge *every* member of his flock to demonstrate their faith by their good works.

The example of Rahab should continue to challenge us today. Sometimes we excuse our lack of good works by using the same argument that James' flock was tempted to use. We look at those in our congregation who are demonstrating their faith in their lives and we assume that they must have some super added gift of faith that we did not receive. We tend to view these people as if they are some type of modern spiritual superheroes. We view them very much like the Jews viewed Abraham. We make our own modern-day 'Abrahams'.

Perhaps the 'Abrahams' in your congregation include that wise and godly retired pastor or that seeming perfect family with nine perfectly behaved children. When we consider these modern-day 'Abrahams' we are tempted to offer this type of argument: 'I can't live like them. I didn't grow up in a Christian home. I lacked spiritual training and guidance. I committed serious sins before my conversion and I still struggle with sin. How can I be expected to live like them? They have something that I simply don't have.' The example of Rahab will not allow us to do this. It will not allow us to fabricate such a two-tiered paradigm of the Christian life. All Christians have received the same gift of faith and all Christians, be they an Abraham or a Rahab, are called to live in a manner which demonstrates that they are recipients of that gift.

## A message for the modern church

As we have seen in this chapter, James and Paul are not at odds with one another regarding the grounds of our justification before God. They were simply addressing different audiences and different issues. Paul was addressing Jewish legalists and was clarifying the issue of how one becomes a Christian. James was addressing Christians who had grown lax in living their faith and was clarifying the need for good works in the life of a believer. Yes, Paul and James have two different messages, but they are complementary rather than contradictory messages. We need to hear the message of both Paul and James on the topic of faith and works.

While the messages of Paul and James are equally important, it is worth asking ourselves which of these messages the modern church needs to hear most. I think the answer to that question is pretty clear. While the doctrine of justification by faith alone is under attack in our day, the main problem faced by evangelical Christianity is not legalism, but rather licence. Our problem is the lack of a living and active faith which produces good works, with the result that we are living well below God's standard of living for us. Dr James Montgomery Boice recognized the widespread nature of this problem in the modern church and wrote the following in the earlier part of his ministry:

> Perhaps there has never been a period in history when true Christians have lived more like those who are in the world and have demonstrated so little of the high standards of the Christian faith.[6]

James' message is desperately needed in the modern church. We need to hear what he has to say to us. We need to hear and heed the warning of James that true saving faith always yields a life which demonstrates that faith. While we must always be defenders of the doctrine of justification by faith alone as set forth by Paul, we must equally defend the teaching of James that this saving faith never remains alone.

Demanding good works from Christians is not in conflict with the Reformation. For example, the *Westminster Confession of Faith*, which so ardently contends for the Reformation doctrine of justification by faith alone, devotes an entire chapter to the necessity of good works in the Christian life.[7] Consider the following words from this chapter of the confession which not only speak of the necessity of good works, but also enumerate the many purposes served by our good works:

> These good works, done in obedience to God's commandments, are the fruits and evidences of a true and lively faith: and by them believers manifest their thankfulness, strengthen their assurance, edify their

brethren, adorn the profession of the Gospel, stop the mouths of the adversaries, and glorify God, whose workmanship they are, created in Christ Jesus thereunto, that, having their fruit unto holiness, they may have the end, eternal life.[8]

Likewise, John Calvin wrote the following words in his commentary on James:

Man is not justified by faith alone, that is by a bare and empty knowledge of God; he is justified by works, that is, his righteousness is known and proved by his fruits.[9]

Finally, even Martin Luther demanded that our faith must produce works. Note how he defined the biblical concept of faith:

Oh, it is a living, busy, active, mighty thing, this faith; and so it is impossible for it not to do good works incessantly. It does not ask whether there are good works to do, but before the question rises; it has already done them, and is always at the doing of them. He who does not these works is a faithless man.[10]

Clearly, the Reformers saw no conflict between the teaching of Paul and James.

James reminds us of the important truth that it is simply not enough to merely believe in the truths of Christianity. James demands that we also live those truths. According to James, a Christian who believes in God, but does not live for God, is no better than a demon. He declares to us in James 2:19: 'You believe that there is one God. Good! Even the demons believe that — and shudder.' James forces us to ask the question: 'Is my faith any better than that of the demons?' The only way to answer that question is by assessing the fruit of our faith. We must examine whether our lives are yielding good deeds. Remember, James tells us that faith without deeds is utterly useless.

The good news is that when we believe in Jesus Christ and become united to him by faith we cannot help but yield the fruit of good works. In John 15:5, Jesus declares the following promise to those who are united to him: 'I am the vine; you are the branches. If a man remains in me and I in him, *he will bear much fruit*,' (emphasis mine). Note carefully the words of Jesus here. He does not say that those who are united to him 'can' or 'may' bear much fruit, but rather he says that those united to him 'will' bear much fruit. Once again James merely echoes the teaching he received from his brother. Like Jesus, James reminds us that bearing fruit is not an option in the Christian life, but rather it is an absolute necessity. So, as the *Westminster Confession* states, begin adorning your profession of the gospel by putting your faith to work.

# 12.

# The power of the tongue

*'All kinds of animals, birds, reptiles and creatures of the sea are*
*being tamed and have been tamed by man, but no man can*
*tame the tongue. It is a restless evil, full of deadly poison'*
(James 3:7-8).

As I write this book, the largest cruise ship in the world is Royal Caribbean's *Freedom of the Seas*. The ship weighs a massive 160,000 tons. It is over 1,000 feet long, around 200 feet wide and slightly over 200 feet tall (that's about the same height as the Statue of Liberty!). The amazing thing is that this colossal vessel, filled with modern engineering marvels, still utilizes an ancient, simple and relatively small instrument to assist in steering it — a rudder.[1]

In the first century, when James wrote his epistle, ships were of course much smaller than *Freedom of the Seas*. However, just like this huge modern ship, those ancient vessels were controlled and directed by a rudder which was small in proportion to the size of the entire vessel. The people to whom James wrote were very familiar with matters of the sea. This is why James frequently makes use of maritime illustrations. As his readers looked at the large vessels of their day, they no doubt marvelled at the fact that these vessels were controlled by their tiny rudders. They probably thought to themselves, 'How could something so small control something so large?'

James drew from his audience's maritime knowledge in order to illustrate for them the tremendous power of the tongue. He told them that their tongue functioned in their lives much like a rudder functions on a ship. Just like that rudder, our tongues have the power to control the entire direction of our lives. In James 3:1-12, James addresses three topics related to the tongue, and each reveals its terrible power. The three topics James tackles are the teacher and the tongue, taming the tongue and two uses of the tongue.

## The teacher and the tongue

As James commences his homily about the power of the tongue he immediately focuses his attention on the role of the tongue in the teaching office of the church. In the opening verse of this section of his epistle James unleashes the following warning: 'Not many of you should presume to be teachers, my brothers, because you know that we who teach will be judged more strictly.' While all Christians will be judged for how they use their tongues, James tells us that teachers of God's Word will be judged according to a much stricter standard.

Why does James launch his homily on the power of the tongue with this one-verse warning regarding the teaching office? The answer to this question is found in James' maritime analogy involving the rudder and the ship.

James understood that in many ways the pastor serves as the rudder of the congregation. Just as the small instrument of the rudder can control the course and direction of the entire ship, so too can one man, the pastor, control the direction of an entire congregation. This is why those who teach in the church are held to a higher standard. James addresses the teaching office first because he understood that just one man can shipwreck a congregation simply by misusing his tongue.

It is quite possible that James' flock had experienced firsthand the devastating effects of the misuse of the tongue in the teaching office. False teachers were prevalent in the early church. The reason for this was that, unlike in our modern world, the teaching office was highly regarded and respected. The Jews held rabbis and scribes in very high esteem and, as these Jews converted to Christianity, they transferred this esteem to the Christian equivalent of these positions. Because the office of teacher was so highly coveted, it often attracted many fraudulent practitioners who were motivated to use this office for selfish ends. Many men pursued the teaching office to acquire personal power, prestige and wealth. These men often led their flocks astray through false doctrine, sophistry, immoral practices and unethical behaviour.

*Subversion or starvation*

James understood the importance of the teaching office and the potential it had to destroy the church. He understood that teachers could destroy their flocks through subversion, by teaching them falsehoods; or through starvation, by failing to feed them the Word of God. These twin problems of subversion and starvation remain with us today, with the latter problem being the greatest enemy in our age. There are too many occupants of the teaching office of the church who are doing everything except feeding the sheep with the Word of God. The great Scottish pastor, William Still, described this lamentable problem:

The ministers who are the greatest failures are not necessarily those who make such havoc of a church that they have to pass on and leave someone else to put humpty-dumpty together again, but the greatest failures are those who, having tried to run Christ's church as a moneymaking racket, a clockwork train, or a social free-for-all, depart and leave a spiritual wilderness behind them, in which the one thing that is not known at all is the Word of God.[2]

The tongue wields terrible power, particularly when it is in the mouth of a teacher in the church.

Because James understood the power resident in the tongue of the teacher, he warns men not to seek this office inappropriately or hastily. He reminds any who do so, that whoever speaks in God's name will be judged more strictly. By issuing this warning to would-be teachers James is also issuing a simultaneous warning to congregations. He is reminding them that there is no more important decision that they can make than that of selecting the man who will employ his tongue to speak in God's name. Your pastor will be the rudder of your congregation; therefore, choose wisely!

## Taming the tongue

After dealing with the very narrow issue of the office of teacher in the first verse of this chapter, James moves on to broaden his focus in James 3:2-8. In these verses, James is addressing all Christians, and he calls every believer to the difficult, but extremely important, task of taming their tongues. The reason that James calls us to tame our tongues is because they can wield terrible power. James informs us that while the tongue may be small in size, it is great in influence. He wants us to see the disproportional power of the tongue, and he gives us three vivid illustrations to help us to grasp this truth.

*The disproportional power of the tongue*

The first illustration James gives us is found in James 3:3 where he compares the power of the tongue to a bit (or bridle) in a horse's mouth: 'When we put bits into the mouths of horses to make them obey us, we can turn the whole animal.' Do you see how this illustration displays the disproportional power of the tongue? Just as the small bit in a horse's mouth allows the rider to control the direction of the horse, so too our tiny tongue can control the direction of our lives. The point is that the tongue is small, but powerful.

James' second illustration of the disproportional power of the tongue is the one we looked at in the introduction to this chapter. In James 3:4, James likens the power of the tongue to a rudder of a ship: 'Or take ships as an example. Although they are so large and are driven by strong winds, they are steered by a very small rudder wherever the pilot wants to go.' Just as the 'very small rudder' of a ship can control the course of the entire vessel, so too our small tongue can control the entire course of our lives. James is telling us again that the tongue is small, but powerful.

James' final illustration comes in James 3:5-6 where he compares the power of the tongue to a spark which ignites a forest fire:

> Likewise the tongue is a small part of the body, but it makes great boasts. Consider what a great forest is set on fire by a small spark. The tongue also is a fire, a world of evil among the parts of the body. It corrupts the whole person, sets the whole course of his life on fire, and is itself set on fire by hell.

James tells us that our tiny tongues can unleash great power. The tongue is small, but powerful.

*The tongue as a weapon of mass destruction*

There is something else to note in the last illustration on the disproportional power of the tongue. While it is similar to the previous two in its main point, there is a slight alteration in its emphasis. This third illustration's similarity with the other two is clear; once again we have a small thing (a spark) exercising a disproportional amount of control over a much larger thing (a forest fire). However, the difference in this last comparison is that James focuses particularly on the destructive power of an untamed tongue.

In the first two illustrations, which compared the tongue to a bit and a rudder, the point was to show us that when we control our tongue we can control the entire course of our lives. However, in his third illustration James shows us the other side of the coin. James shows what can happen when we *fail* to tame our tongues. He displays for us the disproportional destructive power of an untamed tongue. He tells us that one slip of our tongue can result in a conflagration. James does not want us to underestimate the destructive force contained in our tongues. In James 3:6, he warns us that the tongue has the power to corrupt 'the whole person' and set on fire 'the whole course' of our lives. He even associates the fire of the tongue with the destructive fires of hell (3:6). James wants us to understand that while the tongue is small, it can become a weapon of mass destruction. This is why we must endeavour to tame our tongues.

While James does not provide any specific examples of how the tongue can become a weapon of mass destruction, it is not difficult for us to come up with some examples from our own personal experiences. Most of us, at some time in our lives, have been personally burned by the fire of our own untamed tongue or the fire of the untamed tongue of another.

There are numerous ways by which an untamed tongue can spark a forest fire. Our tongue can bring this level of destruction by spewing forth lies, spreading rumours and sowing discord. The destructive power of an untamed tongue has only been enhanced by our modern technological world. E-mail, instant messaging and social networking sites have opened entirely new frontiers for us to unleash the destructive power of our tongues.

## The difficult task of taming the tongue

James wants us to realize that our tongues can become tools for destruction. This is why he demands that we tame our tongues. But James also realizes that taming our tongues is no easy task. Note his words in James 3:7-8: 'All kinds of animals, birds, reptiles and creatures of the sea are being tamed and have been tamed by man, but no man can tame the tongue. It is a restless evil, full of deadly poison.' James recognizes that taming our tongue is a huge task. While humanity has been very successful in taming and domesticating a vast array of animals, it has continually failed to tame the tongue.[3]

So is there any hope for us to tame our tongues? Given James' words that 'no man can tame the tongue', we may think that it is an impossible task. But James never calls us to do something which we are incapable of doing. While he does want us to grasp how difficult a calling this is, he does not believe that it is an impossible task for a follower of Christ. James' point here is that no *natural* man can tame his tongue.

The Greek word translated as 'man' in James 3:7-8 is a generic term which is meant to refer to human nature or to humanity in general.[4] Therefore, what James is telling us is that humans, left to their own nature, are incapable of taming the tongue, but those who are new creations in Christ can progress towards the perfection of which James speaks in James 3:2. In other words, a Christian, through the enlivening power of the Spirit, can learn to tame his tongue and thus keep his 'whole body in check' (James 3:2).

James tells us that if we want to grow in the Christian life then we should begin by learning to discipline and domesticate our own tongues. The value of disciplining our tongues should not be underestimated. Remember, by controlling this small member of our body we can not only save ourselves and others from great pain, but we can also accomplish great things for Christ.[5]

## Two uses of the tongue

As James concludes his homily about the power of the tongue, he addresses two uses of our tongues. Once again this last topic of James reveals the terrible power of the tongue — this little member of our body has the terrible power to both bless God and destroy God's image. What vexes James is the reality that Christians use their tongues to engage in both of these activities. Note his stern words in James 3:9-12:

> With the tongue we praise our Lord and Father, and with it we curse men, who have been made in God's likeness. Out of the same mouth come praise and cursing. My brothers, this should not be. Can both fresh water and salt water flow from the same spring? My brothers, can a fig-tree bear olives, or a grapevine bear figs? Neither can a salt spring produce fresh water.

Here James condemns a duplicitous use of the tongue. He informs us that it is entirely inconsistent for Christians to use their tongue in this dichotomous way. He forcefully denounces this practice by declaring, 'My brothers, this should not be' (James 3:10).[6]

According to James, a Christian who uses his tongue to both bless God and curse his own brother is just as absurd as a spring which yields both fresh water and salt water, a fig tree which bears olives, or a grapevine which bears figs (James 3:11-12). In other words, James is subtly telling us that when we misuse our tongues in this duplicitous manner we are not producing fruit which is consistent with the Christian life.

James, as he so often does, only gives us two options. When it comes to the use of our tongues, we can either use them in a godly way by blessing God and our fellow man, or we can use them in an ungodly way by cursing God and man. There is no middle position. By giving us only two options James challenges us to engage in a personal assessment regarding the use of our tongues. He wants us to ask ourselves which category best describes us. He wants us to ask ourselves questions like: How am I using my tongue? Am I double-tongued? Is my mouth like a spring which produces both fresh water and salt water? What does the fruit of my tongue reveal about the state of my heart? Is my tongue yielding fruit which is consistent with the Christian life? If you are using your tongue to bless God and curse your fellow man then hear and heed the stern words of pastor James: 'My brothers, this should not be.'

## A tale of the tongue: from paradise to Pentecost

In this section of his epistle, James desires us to grasp the terrible power which is resident in our own tongues. He wants us to understand that how we use our tongues matters. He wants us to see the tremendous ramifications which can result from what we say. He is trying to get us to comprehend the spiritual significance of the tongue. We would be wise to heed James' teaching on this subject, because redemptive history supports what James has to say. From cover to cover, the Bible teaches us about the terrible power of the tongue.

For example, step back for a moment into the Garden of Eden. In many ways, the sin of our first parents involved a misuse of the tongue. First, there was Eve's lie to the serpent in which she claimed that God had commanded her and Adam not to touch the tree of the knowledge of good and evil (Genesis 3:3). While God had prohibited them from eating of this tree, he never said anything about touching it, but Eve uses her tongue to disparage God by making his command to appear onerous, unreasonable and unfair. Adam fared no better. He also misused his tongue when he blamed God and his wife for his own sin: 'The man said, "The woman you put here with me — she gave me some fruit from the tree, and I ate it"' (Genesis 3:12). Just think of the massive forest fire which resulted from the spark of these two untamed tongues!

But redemptive history also reveals the power of the tongue for good. While the tongue was involved in the fall of mankind, it was also involved in the redemption of mankind. God promised, through the prophet Isaiah, that one day he would speak to his people through 'strange tongues' (Isaiah 28:11). This was in fact a promise of the worldwide proclamation of the gospel which occurred as a direct consequence of the death and resurrection of Jesus Christ. On the day of Pentecost this promise began to be fulfilled, as fire in the shape of tongues was seen resting on the heads of the apostles. These flaming tongues were symbolic of the power of the Holy Spirit. By the power of the Spirit, the apostles began to speak in 'other tongues' to a group of people from a variety of nations (Acts 2:3-4). This crowd of disparate people stood bewildered because they all heard the gospel preached in their own tongue (Acts 2:6). On that day over 3,000 came to believe in Jesus Christ. They were saved by the power of the Word of God as it was proclaimed by the tongues of men. Just think of the glorious forest fire for good which resulted from the sparks unleashed from the tongues of those twelve men — tongues tamed by the Holy Spirit!

As Christians we must never underestimate how important it is to control the terrible power resident in our tongues. We must learn more and more to employ our tongues for the praise of God and the edification of his image-bearers. We must keep in mind the words of Jesus when he declared, 'What goes into a man's mouth does not make him "unclean" but what comes out of his mouth, that is what makes him "unclean"' (Matthew 15:11). In order to live the Christian life to its fullest we must always remember that the tongue is small, but powerful!

# 13.

# Pride and providence

*'Now listen, you who say, "Today or tomorrow we will go to this or that city, spend a year there, carry on business and make money." Why, you do not even know what will happen tomorrow. What is your life? You are a mist that appears for a little while and then vanishes. Instead, you ought to say, "If it is the Lord's will, we will live and do this or that." As it is, you boast and brag. All such boasting is evil. Anyone, then, who knows the good he ought to do and doesn't do it, sins'*
(James 4:13-17).

I remember quite vividly the stock market bubble of the late 1990s. During those days I was a young attorney working in a large law firm. For the first time in my life I was making 'real' money and I began to invest some of that money in the booming stock market. Back in those days it was very easy to make money in stocks. In fact, it often felt like you couldn't lose in the market, particularly if you invested in a company whose name ended with '.com'. Because of the extraordinary stock market returns during those years many of the lawyers with whom I worked were planning for an early retirement. Admittedly, I also got caught up in the investment frenzy of that time. As I watched my investment account grow during those years I became convinced that my future financial security was guaranteed. I too was making plans for an early retirement. But then things changed drastically.

In March 2000 the stock market bubble burst. Stock prices began to fall precipitously. Some people lost their entire life savings. Dreams were shattered. Boasting ceased. The party was over. The elaborate plans of many people deflated along with the market bubble. My own prideful plans for an early retirement were soon a distant memory.

In James 4:13-17, Pastor James deals with the topic of planning. He contrasts two ways of making plans for the future. The first way is the worldly way of making plans. This involves making plans in prideful self-reliance on our own individual desires and abilities without giving any regard to God's will. The second way is the way of the godly. The godly *do* make plans for the future, but they always humbly submit these plans to God's will and providence. James tells us that when it comes time to make plans for our future we have two options — we can construct our plans on the foundation of our pride, or of God's providence.

## The way of the world: prideful planning

Before we begin to examine how James condemns the prideful planning method of the world, it is important to stress the fact that the Bible does not condemn making plans for the future. In fact, it actually encourages us to do so. For example, Joseph is commended for planning ahead by storing up grain for the years of famine experienced by Israel (Genesis 41:48-49). Proverbs calls us to look to the ant for an example of how to plan ahead for future needs (Proverbs 6:6-8). Jesus encourages us to be wise planners and stewards of resources in the Parable of the Ten Minas (Luke 19:11-27). The apostle Paul was a master planner who carefully mapped out his missionary journeys and church planting efforts (Acts 18:21; 19:21; 20:16; 1 Corinthians 4:19; 16:5-7). The Bible never condemns us for engaging in wise planning, but it does condemn the practice of engaging in planning which is presumptuous and prideful. It is this type of planning that James confronts in James 4:13-14.

James addresses the topic of prideful planning by giving us another of his vivid illustrations. In James 4:13-14, he introduces us to a group of hypothetical self-confident businessmen who are planning their financial future. One can almost imagine these businessmen hunched over a map of the Mediterranean world plotting their profit-making schemes and putting their business plan in motion. We can imagine one of them pointing his finger to the map and saying, 'Tomorrow we will go to this city, establish our operations for a year and we'll make a fortune!' The entire attitude of these men is arrogant and godless. They display an utter lack of humility and their plans are entirely devoid of any mention of God. This is why James responds to them so harshly:

> Now listen, you who say, 'Today or tomorrow we will go to this or that city, spend a year there, carry on business and make money.' Why, you do not even know what will happen tomorrow. What is your life? You are a mist that appears for a little while and then vanishes.

James chastises these arrogant businessmen for their prideful and presumptuous planning, and in so doing he chastises all who follow this worldly way of making plans.

Once again it is important to reiterate that James does not chastise these businessmen for making plans, but rather for making prideful plans. James has no problem with them making a long-range strategic plan for their enterprise; his problem is that they are self-assured and self-centred in their planning.

They do not pray for their plan. They do not search God's Word regarding their plan. They show absolutely no regard for the fact that their plans are entirely dependent on God's will rather than their own planning acumen. James' quarrel with these men is that they are making plans based on prideful presumptions.

Our modern world is replete with examples of the type of prideful planning which James illustrates in this text. We see it all the time, particularly in the world of business. For example, consider the story of the infamous hedge fund named 'Long Term Capital Management' (LTCM). This hedge fund was founded in 1993 by a prestigious group of financial professionals, including two Nobel prize-winning economists. LTCM was run by the best and the brightest minds. They were very confident in their ability to make money while taking on very little risk. In fact, they boasted that they had developed such a sophisticated model for investing that they could effectively reduce their investment risk to zero. These businessmen believed that they were masters of their own destiny and considered their success all but assured. However, things did not go as they had planned. By 1998, LTCM was on the brink of bankruptcy and the United States government had to orchestrate a $3.5 billion bailout package to save it from collapsing. The founders of LTCM thought they could control their own futures and guarantee their success. They said 'we will' be profitable. Just like the businessmen in James' example, they were filled with prideful presumption.

But one doesn't need to be a businessman or a Nobel prize-winning economist to fall victim to the problem of prideful presumption. This is our problem. We are all prone to displaying a similar level of pride in the major decisions that we make in our lives. Like the businessmen in James' example, we too often declare a self-assured 'we will' when we forge our future plans. We say 'we will' marry that person. We say 'we will' take that job. We say 'we will' retire when we're sixty-five. We say 'we will' about so many aspects of our future. In the 'we wills' of our lives we display a prideful attitude which suggests that we believe that we are in control of the future, that we control the success of our plans, and that we control our destiny. We are not so very different from James' prideful businessmen. We too engage in prideful planning. How many of your plans begin with the words, 'I will'?

## The foolishness of prideful planning

In James 4:14, James exposes the foolishness of the prideful planning of these businessmen. He does this by noting that their plan is built on the false premise that they actually have some type of control over future events. James informs these businessmen, who were so confident of the profits they would make in the following twelve months, that they cannot even successfully predict what will happen in the next twenty-four hours: 'Why, you do not even know what will happen tomorrow.'

James further dismantles their hubris by reminding them of the brevity and frailty of their lives. He tells these men that not only can they not predict what will happen tomorrow, but they also cannot even be certain that they will be alive tomorrow: 'What is your life? You are a mist that appears for a little while and then vanishes' (James 4:14). These men who are so assured of their future plans and profits cannot be certain that they will even have a future pulse.

James utterly deflates their prideful premises by reminding them of their finite abilities and the frailty of their lives. We too need to be continually reminded of these two realities. It is only by remembering our finiteness and frailty that we can turn our hubris into humbleness.

What was missing in the planning of these businessmen was what is often missing from our own planning — the reality that only God can determine the future success of our plans. The planning process of these businessmen reveals that they believed in the sovereignty of man rather than the sovereignty of God. What does your planning process reveal about who is sovereign in your life? Are you self-assured, self-reliant and self-confident as you make your plans? Are your plans built on the foundation of prideful presumption? If so, remember the lessons taught by James in this passage. James tells us that such planning is utter foolishness; it is the way of the worldly.

## The way of the godly: providence and our plans

Thus far James has told us how *not* to make plans for the future. He has told us that a Christian must not make plans based on prideful presumption. In James 4:15-16, he shifts his focus to the topic of how we *should* make our plans for the future. In these verses James teaches us how to make our plans in a godly manner. He reveals to us that the godly construct their plans on the foundation of God's providence.

In theology, providence is a word which encapsulates the truth that God is in control of the entire course of the universe and every event which occurs within it. The *Westminster Shorter Catechism* defines God's works of providence as 'his most holy, wise, and powerful preserving and governing all his creatures, and all their actions'.[1] Do you see how embracing this truth should impact how we plan? Anyone who embraces the biblical truth of God's providence will be unable to act with the pride demonstrated by the businessmen in this passage. People who acknowledge God's providence do not make plans by saying, 'We will do this or that', but rather they say, as James notes in James 4:15, '*If it is the Lord's will*, we will live and do this or that' (emphasis mine). James reminds these businessmen, and us, that the godly submit their plans to God's providence rather than to human pride.

Submitting our plans to God's providence helps us to avoid idolatry in our planning. It is very easy for us to worship our own plans. In Bruce Waltke's helpful book, *Finding the Will of God*, he reminds us that while the Bible instructs us to make plans, it does not instruct us to make our plans into an idol. In other words, we must make sure that we are submitting our plans to God rather than submitting ourselves to our plans. So how do we prevent ourselves from creating an idol out of our plans? We do it by adopting the mindset which James describes in James 4:15. We begin with the Lord's will rather than our own will. We begin with 'if', rather than 'when'. Waltke explains the mindset Christians should have when they approach God with their plans: 'Lord, here is what I am planning to do. I think it is the right step. I've prayed about it, read your Word, and sought the wise counsel of others. I believe this is pleasing to you. So if you will, I plan to do this.'[2]

Submitting our plans to God does not mean we cease to use reason when we make our plans. The Bible doesn't call us to engage in a mystical attempt to discern God's will. There is certainly a place for us to employ the minds God gave us and to exercise our sanctified common sense. However, the Bible warns us that we should never become haughty in the exercise of our God-given reason. Our sinful nature can so easily lead us to turn our reason into an idol. James tells us that we can protect ourselves against idolatry in our planning by prefacing our plans with providence, with a heart-felt trust in God which manifests itself in the spoken words 'If the Lord wills'.

## Practising providence

The apostle Paul provides us with an excellent example of one who displayed the type of providential mindset described by James. Paul practised providence. While Paul was inspired by the Holy Spirit and performed miracles, he never adopted an attitude of pride in his planning. Paul's plans were always made in submission to God's will rather than his own. For example, Paul desperately desired to visit the church in Rome. He refers to this desire twice in his epistle to the Romans, but each time he submits this desire to the will of God:

Romans 1:10:       '...I pray that now at last *by God's will* the way may be opened for me to come to you' (emphasis mine).

Romans 15:32:      'so that *by God's will* I may come to you with joy and together with you be refreshed' (emphasis mine).

Paul made similar remarks to the church at Corinth which he also desired to visit:

1 Corinthians 4:19:   'But I will come to you very soon, *if the Lord is willing*' (emphasis mine).

1 Corinthians 16:7:   'I do not want to see you now and make only a passing visit; I hope to spend some time with you, *if the Lord permits*' (emphasis mine).

So even the apostle Paul recognized the importance of submitting his plans to God. His plans were not built on pride, but rather they were built on providence. This is what James is calling all of us to do as we make plans for our future.

The Puritans provide us with another example of providential planning. If you have ever explored the writings of the Puritans, particularly their personal letters, you will note that they had a common practice of signing their letters with the initials 'D.V.' What do these initials mean? They are derived from the Latin phrase *Deo Volente* which means 'God willing'. When the Puritans signed their letters with these initials they were declaring that their plans were not being constructed upon human pride, but rather upon God's providence. James calls us to sign our entire lives with the initials 'D.V.' Instead of prefacing our plans with the prideful 'we will' we should instead preface them with the humble 'if God wills'. This is how we begin to practise providence. Kent Hughes writes:

> *Deo Volente* is to be the constant refrain of our hearts as we conduct the affairs of our lives. 'If God wills' must be written over students' plans — the choice of a life partner, future education, all everyday activities. Older people need to say from the heart, 'If God wills, I will spend my time... If God wills, my children will become... If God wills, I will wake up tomorrow.'[3]

Is this how you approach your planning? Do you begin your planning by saying 'I will' or 'if God wills'? Even more importantly, if you say 'if God wills', do you really mean it, or is it just a trite Christian phrase? Are your plans constructed upon the foundation of human pride or upon God's providence? Is your life signed with *Deo Volente*? Are you practising providence?

## Peace and our plans

In this section of his epistle, James has presented us with two different methods of planning for the future. He informs us that we can either construct our plans with prideful presumption or with humble reliance upon God's providence. The first method of planning James condemns; the second, he commends. James tells us that one of the ways that Christians set themselves apart from the world is the manner in which they make their plans. Unlike the world, Christians are never to boast about what they will do, but rather they are called to display their humility by prefacing all their plans with an attitude of heart which declares, 'If God wills'.

Committing our plans to providence not only demonstrates our humility and our trust in God, but it also brings incredible blessings to us. We live in an age of anxiety. People are concerned about so many things that could impact their future, such as the threat of international terrorism, access to health care, securing their financial future and paying for their children's education. This palpable cultural anxiety is fed by the reality that people are in fear of the future. Often people respond to this fear with the prideful and foolish notion that they can take charge of their future by constructing seemingly foolproof plans. This is worldly behaviour.

Christians, however, have a much more attractive option available to them. Christians know who holds the future. Because they know that God is in control of the future they do not have to live their lives in slavery to fear and anxiety. Instead they have the opportunity to live their lives in peace by trusting in God's providence.

Jesus does not want his children to live their lives in fear, and he tells us that trusting in God's providence is the remedy for our fears. In the Gospel of Matthew, Jesus explains how the doctrine of providence should conquer all our fears about the future: 'Are not two sparrows sold for a penny? Yet not one of them will fall to the ground apart from the will of your Father. And even the very hairs of your head are all numbered. *So don't be afraid*; you are worth more than many sparrows' (Matthew 10:29-31, emphasis mine). Knowing that God is in charge of our plans, and our futures, allows us to alleviate anxiety and experience peace. This is the blessing of providence, and James wants you to know the liberating power of this blessing. Therefore, construct all your plans on the foundation of providence.

# 14.

# The power of prayer

*'Is any one of you in trouble? He should pray. Is anyone happy? Let him sing songs of praise. Is any one of you sick? He should call the elders of the church to pray over him and anoint him with oil in the name of the Lord. And the prayer offered in faith will make the sick person well; the Lord will raise him up. If he has sinned, he will be forgiven. Therefore confess your sins to each other and pray for each other so that you may be healed. The prayer of a righteous man is powerful and effective. Elijah was a man just like us. He prayed earnestly that it would not rain, and it did not rain on the land for three and a half years. Again he prayed, and the heavens gave rain, and the earth produced its crops'*
(James 5:13-18).

Prayer is one of the most neglected areas of the Christian life. There are many reasons for this. First, there is little theological reflection on the topic. Christian bookstores are filled with books on a myriad of subjects, but there are very few which focus on the subject of prayer. Second, our modern mass-media world is not very conducive to cultivating a culture of prayer. Today we are taught to communicate through 'sound bites', e-mails and instant messages. We have very few deep conversations with one another and, not surprisingly, fewer yet with God. Third, and most importantly, we lack a heart for prayer. We simply don't desire to do it, and we sometimes question its purpose, power and efficacy.

James would view our lack of prayer as a serious spiritual problem. He considers prayer as an essential aspect of the Christian life, and demonstrates its importance by making it one of the major themes of his epistle. In fact, he opens and closes his epistle with this topic. He commenced his epistle by calling us to pray for wisdom (1:5-8), and he ends it with another plea for prayer. As James closes his epistle, he instructs us regarding the purposes of prayer, encourages us with the promise of prayer and challenges us to become practitioners of prayer.

## The purposes of prayer

One of the humorous things about being in the ministry is that people often ask you odd questions about God and theology. Sometimes I have been asked silly questions like, 'Did Adam have a belly button?' Other times I have been presented with challenging and complicated questions like, 'If God is good, why does evil exist?' When it comes to the topic of prayer, I am often asked about whether a particular matter is worthy of prayer. For instance, people will ask me, 'Is it OK to pray for my sick dog?' or 'Is it OK to pray that I will pass a test in school?' I frequently respond to these questions by reminding people that God is our heavenly Father and he loves to hear us speak to him about all types of matters which are upon our heart. The list of things we should *not* pray for is very small.

While we do indeed have the privilege of bringing a wide array of matters before God in prayer, there are some weighty matters which should consistently be part of our prayer life, having a greater priority than others. As James begins to discuss this topic he focuses his attention on three such matters. He informs us that we should be praying regularly for those who are suffering, those who are sick and those struggling with sin. According to James, these are the three main purposes of prayer.

*Suffering*

James opens this section on prayer with the following advice: 'Is any one of you in trouble? He should pray' (James 5:13). According to James, one of the purposes of prayer is to bring assistance to those who are experiencing trouble in their lives.

The Greek word which is translated as 'trouble' in verse 13 could also have been translated as 'suffering'. In fact, this is how the verbal form of this word is translated just a few verses earlier in James 5:10 where it is used to refer to the suffering endured by the prophets: 'Brothers, as an example of patience in the face of *suffering*, take the prophets who spoke in the name of the Lord' (emphasis mine). Pastor James was writing to a flock of people who were 'in trouble'. They were experiencing great suffering, and James told them to respond to their suffering through prayer.

Of course, the admonishment James gave to his flock continues to apply to us today. In other words, James tells us that when we encounter suffering and misfortune our first reaction should be to pray to God about it. Is this how you react when suffering enters your life? It is not always how I react when I experience suffering. When I find myself 'in trouble', sometimes my first response is to employ my rational abilities to find the quickest route out of it. I too often sinfully turn to myself, and not to prayer, in times of trouble.

To what or whom do you turn in times of trouble? James tells us that if we are in trouble there is only one place to turn — we should turn to God in prayer. One of the purposes of prayer is to provide assistance to those who are suffering.

*Sickness*

James reveals to us a second purpose of prayer in James 5:14: 'Is any one of you sick? He should call the elders of the church to pray over him and anoint him with oil in the name of the Lord.' One of the purposes of prayer is to bring healing to the sick.[1]

While all Christians should have their prayers peppered with requests for those who are sick, James particularly refers to the role of elders in praying for the sick. It is likely that the circumstance that would call for this type of special elder-led prayer is when a member of the church has become extremely ill. The fact that James calls the elders to 'pray over' the sick person indicates that he is probably unable to get up from his bed.[2] There are times when the shepherds of the church are to demonstrate their pastoral care for the flock by gathering at the bed of a very ill member of their congregation and praying for that person to be healed.[3]

At first glance it appears that James promises, in a formulaic way, that the prayer of the elders over the sick will be met with guaranteed success: 'And the prayer offered in faith will make the sick person well; the Lord will raise him up' (James 5:15).[4] However, James is not offering such a simplistic guarantee in this verse; instead he is declaring that if the one *to whom* the prayer is offered in faith so wills it, he can make the sick person well.[5]

The focus of James' call to pray for the sick is not on the sick person and not on the elders, but it is entirely on the sovereign will of God. It is the Lord, and only the Lord, who can 'raise up' a sick person from his bed and make him well. This is the very reason why we should pray to God for those who are sick, because we know only he can make them well. Therefore, make sure you are praying regularly for those who are sick in your congregation. Make a list of those with physical needs and pray for them daily. The privilege of praying for the sick is not limited to the eldership. It is a privilege which extends to all the priests of the New Covenant, to every believer. One of the purposes of prayer is to bring healing to those who are sick.

*Sin*

James unfolds a third purpose of prayer in James 5:16: 'Therefore confess your sins to each other and pray for each other so that you may be healed.'[6] Here James calls us to use prayer as a means to bring spiritual healing to the wounds caused by our sins. One of the purposes of prayer is to deal with the problem of sin.

Prayer is very versatile when it comes to dealing with our sins. First, we can use prayer to confess our personal and private sins directly to God. We do this in the confines of our personal private prayer times. Second, we can use times of corporate prayer to engage in a confession of our corporate sins to God. We often do this in the context of a worship service. But there is a third way that prayer can be used to deal with our sin. We can use prayer as a means to experience healing and forgiveness in interpersonal relationships within the church. It is to this third function of prayer that James turns his focus in James 5:16.

What James is calling us to do in this verse is consistent with what Jesus calls us to do in Matthew 18. In Matthew 18:15-18, Jesus sets out the steps which are required to resolve disputes between Christians in the church. The first step states: 'If your brother sins against you, go and show him his fault, just between the two of you. If he listens to you, you have won your brother over' (v. 15). Here Jesus tells us that when a brother in the Lord has sinned against us, it is our responsibility to go to our brother and explain the offence. The purpose of this step is to allow the brother who offended an opportunity to repent and receive forgiveness. The ultimate goal of this process is to achieve interpersonal reconciliation, to win 'your brother over'. It is in this context that James 5:16 is to be implemented. As we work out our interpersonal conflicts we should 'confess [our] sins to each other and pray for each other' so that we 'may be healed'. When we follow this biblical pattern, sins are truly forgiven, true healing is experienced and intimate fellowship is fully restored.

Unfortunately, when Christians experience offence from a brother, they often fail to follow these healing steps described by Jesus and James. Instead they foolishly attempt to bottle up their feelings regarding the offence. Instead of dealing with it they let it linger, simmer and fester. Alternatively, sometimes Christians become so outraged over an offence that they skip this first step entirely. Instead of going to the person who offended them, they insist on jumping immediately to the level of official church discipline. Both of these responses only make matters worse and increase the risk of creating serious divisions in the church. The biblical way to respond to an offence, according to Jesus and James, is to go directly to the person who made the offence, receive his confession of sin, reconcile with him and then conclude the meeting by praying for one another.

James tells us that prayer is a means of bringing healing to sin-fractured relationships. It is simply difficult to remain angry with a brother or retain petty grievances against him when you pray for him. Prayer is a healing balm which can be generously applied to the infectious wounds caused by our sins. Prayer allows us a mechanism through which we can receive healing from God for our sins, and it also allows us to experience this healing on a horizontal level as we pray for each other in our churches. Have you been using your prayers to confess your sins? Have you been using prayer as a means of healing the damaged relationships in your church? One of the purposes of prayer is to deal with our sins.

James reveals to us three purposes of prayer. He tells us that prayer has the power to alleviate suffering, bring physical healing and facilitate the forgiveness of sin and the reconciliation of interpersonal relationships. Our world is filled with broken people — people who are broken with suffering, sickness and sin. We need to be praying for them. Our churches are also filled with people who are broken with suffering, sickness and sin. We need to be praying for them too. We also need to be praying for ourselves as we encounter this triad of brokenness. The modern church is in desperate need of recovering the power of prayer.

It is also important for us to evaluate our own personal prayer life by the standard of James' three purposes for prayer. While these three purposes do not exhaust the proper subject matter of prayer, they should serve as pillars in our prayer lives; that is, these three subjects should predominate in our prayers. Do they predominate in your prayer life or is it governed by personal desires and material gain? James tells us that a godly prayer life is filled with requests for the alleviation of suffering, the healing of the sick and the forgiveness of sins.

## The promise of prayer

After showing us three of the main purposes for prayer, James changes gear in the middle of James 5:16 and addresses a new topic — the efficacy of our prayers. He sums up his homily on prayer with an encouragement to pray, providing us with this promise: 'The prayer of a righteous man is powerful and effective.' James informs us that our prayers are not offered in vain, but contain real power and are an effective means of addressing suffering, sickness and sin.

But perhaps you are thinking that James has qualified this promise by making it conditional on the righteousness of the one praying. In a sense this is true; James *does* add a qualification by noting that 'The prayer of a *righteous* man is powerful and effective.' At first glance it may seem that James is limiting this promise to some type of super-spiritual Christian; but this is not his intent. James knows that every Christian is a righteous man before God because every Christian possesses the imputed righteousness of Christ. Accordingly, when James uses the phrase 'righteous man' he is referring to every believer. The promise of this prayer is made to all Christians.

*The illustration of Elijah*

That James is applying this promise regarding the power of prayer to every believer is supported by the illustration he uses in James 5:17-18. In these verses, James uses the Old Testament prophet Elijah to support the point he is trying to make about the power and efficacy of prayer. Note how he describes Elijah's qualifications as he introduces his illustration: '*Elijah was a man just like us*. He prayed earnestly that it would not rain, and it did not rain on the land for three and a half years. Again he prayed, and the heavens gave rain, and the earth produced its crops' (emphasis mine). James describes Elijah as 'a man just like us'. That is a very interesting way to introduce such a famous figure. For instance, James could have introduced Elijah as follows: 'Elijah was a great Old Testament prophet who performed amazing miracles.' But James does not do this. Instead he focuses on Elijah's similarity to us.

Why does James introduce Elijah in this manner? He does this because he wants us to see that our prayers are no different than those offered by that great prophet. It is important to remember that Elijah, while a great prophet, also experienced many spiritual valleys. He was a 'righteous man', but he was far from a perfect man. Daniel Doriani writes the following of Elijah:

> Like us, he served from a position of weakness. He felt the world's powers arrayed against him. He was prone to despair. He was not worthy, he was simply a righteous man who prayed, for individuals and for his society.[7]

Elijah was a man just like us.

The illustration of Elijah supports the idea that *every* believer is righteous before God and *every* believer can cling to the promise that our prayers are both powerful and effective. Sometimes our prayer lives begin to languish because we come to doubt the efficacy and power of prayer. After all, many of our prayers seem to go unanswered for years and many are answered in ways contrary to our petitions. It is very easy for us to succumb to the belief that praying is a waste of time. James provides a remedy to such thinking. He lifts up the hearts of his people with the promise that our prayers are powerful and effective. He tells us that prayer is a God-ordained means to change things that seem unchangeable. James states that it was through prayer that Elijah saw changes in things that only God could change, like whether it will rain or not. As J. A. Motyer notes:

> The general truth which James is drawing out of the history of Elijah is expressed in verse 17: human prayer, divine results. To withhold rain is something only God can do... God the Creator orders the life of the world in the light of the prayers of his people.[8]

The promise of prayer is that it is a powerful and effective means of addressing seemingly unchangeable human circumstances. This promise is all the more glorious when we remember that it is a promise given to every Christian.

## Becoming a practitioner of prayer

James concludes his letter with a grand exposition on the power of prayer. He reveals to us the amazing things which prayer can effectively and powerfully address: suffering, sickness and sin. He also tells us that the amazing power of prayer is available to all believers. Shouldn't knowing these realities fill us with an insatiable desire to pray? That's what James expected them to do. He expected his flock to respond to his homily on prayer by praying! He expected them to become practitioners of prayer.

Becoming a practitioner of prayer is not a difficult task. God did not make speaking to him a complicated matter. There are no special formulas. There is also no special appointed time for prayer. We can pray at all times and at any time. Finally, there is also no need for an earthly mediator to pray on our behalf. Every Christian has direct and immediate access to the Father through the work of Jesus our great High Priest. The only thing necessary to become a practitioner of prayer is a heart that desires to commune frequently with God. Do you have such a heart? If you do, then you will make time in your life for prayer. You will become a practitioner of prayer.

What James is trying to teach us in this part of his letter is that prayer is part of the warp and woof of the Christian life. He sees prayer as an appropriate response to every event in our life. This is why he followed the question, 'Is any one of you in trouble? He should pray,' with the question, 'Is anyone happy? Let him sing songs of praise' (James 5:13). Whether we are 'in trouble' or 'happy', our response should be similar — we should direct our hearts to God in prayer and praise. Every Christian should be an active practitioner of prayer.

Finally, becoming a practitioner of prayer has tremendous blessings. James tells us that prayer can help us, and others, through suffering, sickness and sin. He reminds us that prayer is effective for these things. Are these not the things that so frequently trouble your own heart? People in our culture are grasping for every possible ineffective remedy for their suffering, sickness and sin. Christians do not have to engage in such desperate measures. All we have to do is go to our loving Father and pray about them. The ultimate blessing of being a person of prayer is the peace which comes from knowing that God hears and answers our prayers.

It is quite fitting that James ends his letter with an emphasis on prayer, because he was a man of prayer. For example, one ancient church historian wrote the following of James:

> But James the brother of the Lord, who, as there were many of this name, was surnamed the Just by all... He was in the habit of entering the temple alone, and was often found upon his bended knees, and interceding for the forgiveness of the people; so that his knees became as hard as a camel's, in consequence of his habitual supplication and kneeling before God.[9]

When it comes to prayer in the Christian life we should not only follow James' words, but also his example. Be like James. Become a practitioner of prayer.

# Notes

## Chapter 1

1. As quoted in Douglas J. Moo, *The Letter of James* (Grand Rapids, MI: Eerdmans, 2000), p.5.
2. James Adamson, *The Epistle of James: NICOT* (Grand Rapids, MI: Eerdmans, 1976), p.18.
3. The six are: James the Son of Zebedee (Mark 1:19; Acts 1:13), James the Son of Alphaeus (Mark 3:18; Acts 1:13), James the Younger (Mark 15:40), James the father of Judas (Luke 6:16; Acts 1:13), James the brother of Jesus (Mark 6:3; Acts 12:11; 15:13; 21:18; Gal. 1:19; 2:9, 12; 1 Cor. 15:1), James the brother of Jude (Jude 1).
4. Douglas Moo notes the following similarities between the epistle of James and the speech of James recorded in Acts 15: 'The epistolary "greeting" (Gk. *chairein*) occurs in Jas. 1:1 and Acts 15:23, but in only one other place in the NT; the use of "name" (*onoma*) as the subject of the passive form of the verb "call" (*kaleo*) is peculiar, yet is found in both Jas. 2:7 and Acts 15:17; the appeal "listen, my brothers" occurs in both Jas. 2:5 and Acts 15:13; and several other, less striking, similarities are also found.' Douglas J. Moo, *The Letter of James*, p.10. For an exhaustive comparison see James B. Mayor, *Epistle of Saint James* (Grand Rapids, MI: Zondervan, 1954), pp.iii-iv.

5. The other strongest candidate for authorship is James the Son of Zebedee. This James was an apostle and was one of the original 12. However, he was martyred in A.D. 44 (recorded in Acts 12:1-12), and it is very unlikely that the epistle of James was written before A.D. 44. Regarding the audience of the epistle, James the Lord's brother would be perfectly suited to address Jews who were dispersed from Jerusalem.

6. Daniel M. Doriani, *James: REC* (Philipsburg, NJ: P & R, 2007), p.5.

7. As above, p.5, cited in footnote 4.

8. J. A. Motyer, *The Message of James: The Bible Speaks Today*, ed. John R. W. Stott (Downers Grove, IL: IVP, 1985), p.11.

9. As above, p.11.

10. Thomas Manton, *James* (Carlisle, PA: Banner of Truth, reprinted 1998), p.13.

11. As above, p.13.

## Chapter 2

1. James Adamson, *The Epistle of James*, p.18. James' unique vocabulary also reflects his knowledge and reliance on the Septuagint, the Greek version of the Old Testament. Forty-six of the seventy-three unique words used by James in his epistle appear in the Septuagint.

2. Daniel M. Doriani provides a helpful comparison between James and Proverbs in his commentary. See Doriani, *James*, p.9.

3. For a full discussion of the nature of the wisdom of James and how it differs from Old Testament wisdom see John A. Burns, 'James, the Wisdom of Jesus', *Criswell Theological Review*, 1:1, (1986), pp.113-135.

4. Dennis E. Johnson, *Him We Proclaim* (Philipsburg, NJ: P & R Publishing, 2007), p.369.

5. See Amos 5:11-12; Micah 2:1-3; and Zephaniah 1:12-14.

6. Moo, *The Letter of James*, p.1.

7. D. Edmond Hiebert, 'The Unifying Theme of the Epistle of James', *Bibliotheca Sacra*, vol. 135 (July 1978), p.231.

8. The scholar is James D. G. Dunn. The quote is cited in Dennis E. Johnson, *Him We Proclaim*, p.370.

9. See Donald Guthrie, *New Testament Introduction* (Downers Grove, IL: IVP, 1990), pp.729-730, for a helpful comparison between the contents of James and the Sermon on the Mount. See also Peter H. Davids, *The Epistle of James: NIGTC* (Grand Rapids, MI: Eerdmans, 1982), pp.47-48, and Virgil V. Porter, 'The Sermon on the Mount in the Book of James, Part I', *Bibliotheca Sacra*, vol. 162, no. 647, July-September 2005, pp.344-60.
10. Moo, *The Letter of James*, p.7.
11. Luke Timothy Johnson, *Brother of Jesus, Friend of God: Studies in the Letter of James* (Grand Rapids, MI: Eerdmans, 2004), p.22.
12. Motyer, *James*, p.14.

## Chapter 3

1. Motyer, *James*, p.31.
2. Moo, *The Letter of James*, p.55.
3. Peter H. Davids, *The Epistle of James: NIGTC* (Grand Rapids, MI: Eerdmans, 1982), p.70.

## Chapter 4

1. R. Kent Hughes, *James: Faith That Works* (Wheaton, IL: Crossway, 1991), p.18.
2. See also Romans 5:3 and 2 Corinthians 7:4.
3. John Calvin, *Calvin's Commentaries*, vol. 22 (Grand Rapids, MI: Baker Books, 1989), pp.279-280.
4. Moo, *The Letter of James*, p.229.

## Chapter 5

1. In fact, some scholars number over 300 uses of *sophia* in the Septuagint. See Edwin Hatch and Henry A. Redpath, *A Concordance to the Septuagint*, vol. 2 (Grand Rapids, Baker 1983), pp.1278-81.
2. A form of the word *sophia* is used seven times in Exodus 31-36.
3. James Adamson, *The Epistle of James*, p.56.

## Chapter 6

1. The term 'double-minded' is actually one word in the original Greek — *dipsychos*. *Dipsychos* literally means 'double-souled'. Many scholars think that James coined this word. He is the only NT author who uses it, employing it a second time in James 4:8.
2. Moo, *The Letter of James*, p.63.
3. As quoted in R. Kent Hughes, *James: Faith That Works*, p.30.
4. Adamson, *The Epistle of James*, p.58.
5. Doriani, *James: REC*, pp.25-6.
6. Moo, *The Letter of James*, p.60.
7. Motyer, *James*, pp.37-38.
8. The facts regarding Hoyt's story were drawn from the article 'Strongest Dad in the World' by Rick Reilly, which appeared in the 15 June 2005 issue of *Sports Illustrated* magazine.
9. There is a stirring video displaying the courage of the Hoyts available at www.youtube.com.
10. R. Kent Hughes, *James: Faith That Works*, p.25.
11. Davids, *The Epistle of James: NIGTC*, p.72.

## Chapter 7

1. G. K. Chesterton, *Orthodoxy* (Wheaton, IL: Harold Shaw Publishers, 1994), p.86.
2. As above, p.85.
3. As above, p.85.
4. For example, see Galatians 6:13; Ephesians 2:9; Romans 2:23; 1 Corinthians 1:29; and 2 Corinthians 5:12.
5. Davids, *The Epistle of James*, p.76.
6. The imagery of a fading flower to describe brevity and temporality is a common one in the Old Testament. See Psalm 103:15-16 and Isaiah 40:6-8.
7. James Montgomery Boice, *Psalms*, vol. 2 (Grand Rapids, MI: Baker, 1996), p.411.
8. As above.
9. Here James once again echoes the words of Jesus in the Sermon on the Mount, 'Do not store up for yourselves treasures on earth, where moth and rust destroy, and where thieves break in and steal. But store up for yourselves treasures in heaven, where

# Notes

moth and rust do not destroy, and where thieves do not break in and steal,' (Matthew 6:19-20).

10. Motyer, *James*, p.44.
11. Chesterton, *Orthodoxy*, p.86.
12. As above.

## Chapter 8

1. The noun 'trial' (*peirasmos*) from James 1:12 and the verbs 'tempted', 'tempting' and 'tempt' are all related words in the original Greek. This Greek word group can be translated as 'trial' or 'temptation'. The word 'trial' connotes outward struggles with circumstances and the word 'temptation' connotes inward struggles with sin. Context determines which translation is appropriate. The context in James 1:12-18 makes it clear that James is referring specifically to the inward struggle with sin and thus he is dealing with the matter of temptation.
2. James' unequivocal statement that God is not the source of our temptations may seem a bit confusing in light of the Lord's Prayer. After all, in the Lord's Prayer we petition God to 'not lead us into temptation' (Matthew 6:13; and Luke 11:4). If God is not the source of our temptations then why do we ask him to not lead us into them? The answer to this question is found in the previous note where we saw that the translation of the Greek word *peirasmos* may be either 'trial' or 'temptation'. The word *peirasmos* in the Lord's Prayer is most likely referring to trials and perhaps specifically to those trials experienced at the end of the age. See Donald Hagner's commentary on Matthew for more information: Donald A. Hagner, *Matthew 1-13: Word Biblical Commentary*, vol. 33A (Dallas, Texas: Word, 1993), pp.151-2.
3. Davids, *The Epistle of James*, p.82.
4. Peter H. Davids provides a helpful analysis of the meaning of these words. See *The Epistle of James*, p.84.
5. D. Edmond Hiebert, *The Epistle of James* (Chicago, IL: Moody, 1979), pp.107-8.
6. This illustration of Amnon is referenced in my book on marriage, *What the Bible Teaches About Marriage* (Evangelical Press, 2007), pp.49-50.
7. Doriani, *James*, p.42.

**Chapter 9**

1. There are many good Bible reading programmes available on the Internet. Simply go to a search engine (like Google or Yahoo) and type in 'Bible reading plans'. One helpful plan is offered by The Navigators at their website: www.navigators.org.
2. Motyer, *James*, p.70.

**Chapter 10**

1. There is a debate among scholars regarding the setting of this example. Some scholars believe that the 'meeting' in verse two refers to the gathered assembly in worship. Others believe that it is a judicial situation in which the church is exercising church discipline. This latter interpretation is supported by the reference to judgement in verse four ('and become *judges* with evil thoughts').
2. In his commentary on James, Daniel Doriani suggests that the sin of partiality, or favouritism, actually directly violates each of the Ten Commandments. See Doriani, *James*, pp.72-3.

**Chapter 11**

1. The five '*solas*' are five Latin phrases used by the Protestant Reformers to articulate the core emphases of the Reformation. They include the following: a) *sola Scriptura* ('Scripture alone'), which emphasizes that Scripture alone is to guide the believer in doctrine and life; b) *sola fide* ('faith alone'), which emphasizes that the gift of faith is the sole instrument, or means, by which justification is imputed to believers; c) *sola gratia* ('grace alone'), which emphasizes that the believer's justification is entirely dependent on the unmerited favour of God and is not due to any inherent righteousness in the believer; d) *solus Christus* ('Christ alone'), emphasizing that Jesus Christ is the sole mediator of justification; e) *soli Deo gloria* ('glory of God alone'), emphasizing that all glory and praise for our salvation is attributable to God and to him alone.
2. Alexander Ross, *The Epistles of James and John: NICOT* (Grand Rapids, MI: Eerdmans, 1954), p.53. As quoted in Hiebert, *The Epistle of James*, p.174.

3. Paul frequently refers to the following sections of Genesis which deal with promises made to Abraham: 12:1-4; 15:1-6 and 18.
4. First-century Jews regarded women as innately inferior to men.
5. John Calvin, *Calvin's Commentaries*, vol. xxii, trans. and ed. by John Owen (Grand Rapids, MI: Baker, 1989), p.316.
6. James M. Boice, *Philippians: An Expositional Commentary* (Grand Rapids, MI: Zondervan, 1971), p.101.
7. Chapter 16 of the *Westminster Confession of Faith* is entitled 'Of Good Works'.
8. *Westminster Confession of Faith* 16:1. The confession includes James 2:18 as a supporting text for the statement, 'These good works, done in obedience to God's commandments, are the fruits and evidences of a true and lively faith.'
9. Calvin, *Calvin's Commentaries*, vol. xxii, p.316.
10. As quoted in R. Kent Hughes, *James: Faith That Works*, p.122. This quote is originally from the preface to Luther's commentary on the book of Romans.

## Chapter 12

1. This modern vessel of course employs many other devices to steer it. It requires more than a simple rudder.
2. William Still, *The Work of the Pastor* (Carlisle, Cumbria, UK: Paternoster Publishing, 1996), p.23.
3. Many commentators believe that James is making a direct allusion to the creation mandate of Genesis 1:26 by referring to 'All kinds of animals, birds, reptiles and creatures of the sea' in James 3:7. This four-fold division of animal kingdom is also present in the creation account.
4. Motyer, *James*, p.124.
5. If you long to control your tongue, read through the book of Proverbs and meditate on its wisdom regarding this issue.
6. James gives examples of the good and bad uses of the tongue in his letter. For instance, in James 5:19-20 he displays how we can use our tongue in a good way by turning our brother away from sin. On the other hand, in James 4:11-12, James shows us we can use our tongues for evil by slandering our brother.

**Chapter 13**

1. *Westminster Shorter Catechism*, Q & A 11.
2. Bruce K. Waltke, *Finding the Will of God* (Grand Rapids, MI: Eerdmans, 1995), p.125.
3. Kent Hughes, *James: Faith That Works*, p.206.

**Chapter 14**

1. Some commentators have argued that the sickness being referred to here is spiritual in nature, but the grammar and context do not support this conclusion.
2. The conclusion that this sick person was bedridden is also supported by the promise that the Lord will 'raise him up' in James 5:15.
3. When James calls the elders to pray for the sick he also calls them to anoint the sick person with oil. Many people wonder about the purpose of the oil, and scholars have long debated its meaning and significance. Most likely the purpose of the oil was to consecrate the sick person to God. Oil was frequently used in the Old Testament to symbolically set apart prophets, priests and kings to God, and it is likely that this is part of the symbolic meaning of the oil here. It is also possible that the oil serves as a symbol of the work of the Holy Spirit. James calls the elders to symbolically set apart the sick to the healing powers of the Great Physician and his Holy Spirit. In essence, the oil takes the focus off the elders as the healers and places it solely on God as the healer of the sick.
4. This passage has provided great fodder for the 'faith-healers' of our age who often claim that the only reason sick people fail to be healed is because of their personal lack of faith in asking for healing. Is this what James is teaching here? Let me suggest two reasons why this text does *not* support the teaching of the 'faith-healers'. First, James does not say that a prayer offered with sufficient *personal* faith will bring healing. In fact, he doesn't even mention the faith of the sick person. The 'prayer offered in faith' is not offered by the sick man, but rather by the elders. Second, the phrase 'prayer offered in faith' is not referring to the faith of the elders, but rather it is referring to the one *in whom* the elders are placing their faith. The focus is

not on the elders' subjective faith, but rather it is on the object of their faith — God.

5. It is noteworthy that James declares that the Lord will 'raise up' the sick person. James may be deliberately intending us to grasp a double meaning in the phrase 'raise up'. That is, James may be saying that the sick may *either* be raised up in this life through physical healing or they may be healed on the last day when they are raised up in the resurrection of the dead and receive their new and glorious body.

6. Some commentators suggest that James 5:16 is simply a continuation of James 5:14-15 involving the issue of physical healing. There certainly is some continuity between the verses, and sin and sickness were often linked together in the ancient world, but I am convinced James 5:16 introduces a new topic. For instance, one of the indicators of a new topic is the clear transition from elder-led prayer in James 5:14-15 to mutual prayer in James 5:16. Also, James changes his focus to sin rather than sickness.

7. Doriani, *James*, p.201.

8. Motyer, *James*, p.207.

9. This quote is from the church historian Hegesippus and was recorded in Eusebius' *Ecclesiastical History*, 2:23.

A wide range of Christian books is available from Evangelical Press. If you would like a free catalogue please write to us or contact us by e-mail. Alternatively, you can view the whole catalogue online at our web site:

**www.evangelicalpress.org.**

Evangelical Press
Faverdale North, Darlington, DL3 0PH, England

e-mail: sales@evangelicalpress.org

Evangelical Press USA
P. O. Box 825, Webster, New York 14580, USA

e-mail: usa.sales@evangelicalpress.org